T0295678

# Entrepreneurship Development in India

Entrepreneurship development is a major area of focus today as it has huge potential in creating jobs and self-employability and thus contributing to economic development. India, in the last few years in particular, has seen exponential growth of start-ups and new-age entrepreneurs. Both the Central and State Governments have been taking proactive steps towards the development of entrepreneurship in the country. The Government has launched various schemes and programmes to attract investors and create a healthy ecosystem for entrepreneurship. India is one of the largest homes of start-ups in the world and has been highly successful in bringing significant amounts of foreign direct investment. Moreover, the Government is taking active steps in removal of the bureaucratic hurdles and bottlenecks, so that entrepreneurship development is encouraged. In order to promote the culture of entrepreneurship development, the subject has been made part of the curriculum at both undergraduate and postgraduate levels across disciplines.

This book is a sincere attempt to build the fundamentals of the subject amongst students alongside motivating them to become future entrepreneurs. It will be of interest to researchers, academics, and students in the fields of business administration, management, and entrepreneurship.

**Debasish Biswas** is Assistant Professor and Head in the Department of Business Administration at Vidyasagar University, West Bengal, India.

**Chanchal Dey** is Assistant Professor in the Department of Humanities in the College of Engineering and Management at Kolaghat, West Bengal, India.

# Routledge Focus on Business and Management

The fields of business and management have grown exponentially as areas of research and education. This growth presents challenges for readers trying to keep up with the latest important insights. *Routledge Focus on Business and Management* presents small books on big topics and how they intersect with the world of business research.

Individually, each title in the series provides coverage of a key academic topic, whilst collectively, the series forms a comprehensive collection across the business disciplines.

**Rethinking Organizational Culture**
Redeeming Culture through Stories
*David Collins*

**Management in the Non-Profit Sector**
A Necessary Balance between Values, Responsibility and Accountability
*Renato Civitillo*

**Fearless Leadership**
Managing Fear, Leading with Courage and Strengthening Authenticity
*Morten Novrup Henriksen and Thomas Lundby*

**Clusters, Digital Transformation and Regional Development in Germany**
*Marta Götz*

**Entrepreneurship Development in India**
*Debasish Biswas and Chanchal Dey*

For more information about this series, please visit: www.routledge.com/ Routledge-Focus-on-Business-and-Management/book-series/FBM

# Entrepreneurship Development in India

**Debasish Biswas and Chanchal Dey**

Routledge
Taylor & Francis Group

NEW YORK AND LONDON

First published 2021
by Routledge
605 Third Avenue, New York, NY 10158

and by Routledge
2 Park Square, Milton Park, Abingdon, Oxon, OX14 4RN

*Routledge is an imprint of the Taylor & Francis Group, an informa business*

© 2021 Debasish Biswas and Chanchal Dey

*Library of Congress Cataloging-in-Publication Data*
Names: Biswas, Debasish, author. | Dey, Chanchal, author.
Title: Entrepreneurship development in India / Debasish Biswas
    and Chanchal Dey.
Description: New York, NY : Routledge, 2021. | Series: Routledge
    focus on business and management | Includes bibliographical
    references and index.
Identifiers: LCCN 2021003683 (print) | LCCN 2021003684
    (ebook) | ISBN 9780367762193 (hardback) | ISBN 9780367762216
    (paperback) | ISBN 9781003165996 (ebook)
Subjects: LCSH: Small business—India. | Entrepreneurship—India. |
    New business enterprises—India. | Industrial policy—India. |
    Economic development—India.
Classification: LCC HD2346.I5 B569 2021 (print) | LCC HD2346.I5
    (ebook) | DDC 338/.040954—dc23
LC record available at https://lccn.loc.gov/2021003683
LC ebook record available at https://lccn.loc.gov/2021003684

ISBN: 978-0-367-76219-3 (hbk)
ISBN: 978-0-367-76221-6 (pbk)
ISBN: 978-1-003-16599-6 (ebk)

Typeset in Times New Roman
by Apex CoVantage, LLC

This book is dedicated to the readers

# Contents

# Figures

# Tables

# Foreword

## Entrepreneurship: The Context and the Emergence

The world of business and commerce takes shape across entities in organised and unorganised manner spread across the societies, markets, and nations. Initiatives to build organised entities contribute vital into the system to make the system run and continue on principles of dynamic interaction and ongoing exchange of products and services in the marketplace. The role of an entrepreneur becomes very significant in developing the market and sustaining the process of value creation supporting the stream of demands either expressed or dormant. It has been a matter of debate whether an entrepreneur is born or made; however, inputs to the nitty-gritties of formation, maintenance, and growth of entrepreneurial activities create a certitude towards managing and maintaining balance in the world of business. An academic work on entrepreneurship thereby contributes to not only generation of ideas but also making of the new entity to join the race of the corporate world existing heather unto.

Learning from the art of managing enterprises constitutes the science of management, whereas the major decision matrix, methods, approaches, objectives, and functional spreads for decision-making and execution depend upon human intervention using the art of human interactions, deriving ideas, and developing a pattern out of that contributes to the overall scientific process in corporate management. Whether it is in the field of nascent organisation, a de novo idea or a patent formulation, wherever it comes to make an application in the field of work and world, it requires systematic approach to develop a connection among different and varied points contributing to effective decisions and winning actions. Entrepreneurship plays one of the most important roles in this aspect and gradually has evolved to become an important element in the domain of managing the enterprise. Organisations varying across people cultures, national conditionality, product and process varieties, and a wide spread of customer choices-tests-preferences across the globe requires a homogeneous and consistent intervention to scale up the activities in the right manner and drive the corporate activities towards creating a unique mix of efficiency and effectiveness. A new enterprise, thus, begets the legacy of the past and existing to infuse and thrive a new dimension of the corporate work and culture in the future.

Machine power in the manufacturing process and the intervention of tools, technologies, instruments, and digitalisation makes the world of business terminating into the divides of composite human attributes and unified machine culture. While analysing the patterns of civilisations, the great historian Arnold J. Toynbee has identified human civilisation as intellect-driven entities combining together to constantly reinvent a new opening for illumined space in the world. The human process has been categorised as an individual driving his or her realm of life in the way absolutely identified within, the societies and groups of people creating cultures and social trends developing into an overall pattern for their responses and responsiveness through the collective mind-identified thereunto. The most ancient civilisation in the world, the 'Vedic Civilisation' of India had embraced the principles of 'work alone, work for winning, work for distributive benefits, and work for perfection'. This had highlighted:

- Work alone—Principles of work for the sake of work. This concept stimulates thoughts and aspirations of individuals or groups of people towards creating homogenous work to develop and do something fresh and new to benefit the society and the world.
- Work for winning—Work culminating into the total fulfilment of the original objectives set for it. The inspiration to take the new activity forward reaches at its peak when the individual does the work without a selfish motive involved in it. This entrepreneur is actually the most sustainable and beneficial to the world.
- Work for distributive benefits—The outcome of work to be distributed across the human society and the world towards maximising the well-being of every human being and all creatures. Thereby the entrepreneur contributes positive effects towards making society and the world a better place.
- Work for perfection—Work has to be driven down to the culminating end of it, wherein the context, content, and the output of the work becomes fully illumined in the context set for the work. There should be a total appreciation of the context of the work on one hand and the content of the work on the other to benefit the individuals, organisations, and the society at large.

Starting from the concept of the 'work alone' until the 'work for perfection' each step of the work requires a careful understanding of the segments of the work and thereby making the work transformed to the level of a holly work, considered to be the contribution of the person doing the work in the context of the world. A person or a group of people willing to accomplish that requires to possess a bent of mind inquisitive enough to understand the connectivity between and among the elements of work over the period of time.

Entrepreneurial activities require to possess the inquisitive mind, as has been identified during the ancient period, and as an element of scientific orientation to the systems, structures, and procedures available in the world. It is in this context, the entrepreneur needs to have a thorough understanding of the mind and psyche of customers, available purchasing power among people and dynamics of the market networks and the marketing capabilities available in general and with specific reference to products and services on offer. Research emerges out of it. Research orients itself, as a subject and as a notion, towards collecting and collating the elements of work by applying the elements of observations in the context of the work. Modern methods have contributed immensely towards that. Statistical and mathematical approaches to identify the aspects of work are clubbed under the subject title of Entrepreneurial Research Methodology. This ideally involves and includes the following domains and dimensions:

- Understanding the fundamentals of the context of work.
- Understanding the features and processes adopted by the people involved in the work.
- Identifying the mental trends and psychological features through the behavioural aspects of people involved in the context either on the supply side or in the demand side.
- Collecting and collating the elements of the decision matrix for contributing effective decision support systems and strategic considerations to start, run, and maintain business across the globe.
- To identify the potentials within the material, financial, and human resources available in the organisation and prospective contributions by elements in the market and in the society.

It is in this context, understanding and developing a proper perception through categorical learning of the subject of entrepreneurship connected with management functions and processes becomes very important not only in the corporate context but also in the context of human behaviour in any composite of human beings.

I have gone through the highlighting positions of the book titled 'Entrepreneurship Development in India', Routledge Publications, authored by Dr. Debasish Biswas and Mr. Chanchal Dey and have found a unique mix of conceptual grounding and connecting the concepts with the practice through real-world examples, references, cases, explanations, endnotes, and analysis. The work is very lucid but extremely rich in content. Both the authors are very competent from an academic point of view and are highly conversant with the subject of entrepreneurship, particularly in Indian context. Dr. Debasish Biswas has a very wide experience in teaching the subject in diversified forums at the University and Corporate level. He possesses unique qualities of teaching and presenting a subject in a way that is perceived and understood by most people. Anybody accepting this work as either a text or a reference would benefit profusely at any segment of his or her work and thoughts with respect to the corporate world. It is useful for the beginners of the subject, those who are in the midst of the subject as a teacher or learner, those who are into the profile and planning to become an entrepreneur and finally those who are practitioners in business and corporate world as manager-entrepreneur would squarely benefit out of the presentations and content of the work.

I fully recommend this book to all relevant students, teachers, and practitioners throughout.

Thanks to all concerned!

**Prof. (Dr.) R. P. Banerjee**
Chairman & Director, EIILM-Kolkata
Formerly with IIM-Calcutta &
Visited and lectured over a dozen
universities in USA and Europe
Date: 4 January 2021

# Preface

Entrepreneurship is gaining prominence over the past few years and the subject has been introduced in the grassroots level as well. The main objective of writing the book is to present the subject matter in an appealing way to the readers, so that it helps the learners to develop insights about the subject and also to raise awareness about the present landscape of entrepreneurship in the country.

Entrepreneurship development is one of the major areas of focus today as it has huge potential in creating jobs and self-employment and thus contributing to economic development. India, in the last few years, has seen exponential growth of start-ups and new-age entrepreneurs. Both the Central and State Governments have been taking proactive steps towards the development of entrepreneurship in the country. The Government has launched various schemes to attract investors and create a healthy ecosystem for entrepreneurship. At present, India is one of the largest homes of start-ups in the world. Entrepreneurship is seen with lots of pragmatism these days. Moreover, the Government is also taking active steps in removal of the bureaucratic hurdles and bottlenecks, so that entrepreneurship development is encouraged. In order to promote the culture of entrepreneurship development, the subject has been made part of the curriculum at both undergraduate and postgraduate levels across disciplines.

We feel great pleasure in placing the first edition of this book which is the outcome of a great deal of encouragement from our colleagues and students. Our book is a sincere attempt to build the fundamentals of the subject amongst the students alongside motivating them to become future entrepreneurs. This book is appropriate for the learners of entrepreneurship development studying across different levels in colleges and universities. The book will also help the researchers and prospective entrepreneurs to develop a conceptual hindsight of entrepreneurship development in India. We welcome suggestions from the esteemed teachers and our students for enrichment and improvement of the book in the future.

Dr. Debasish Biswas
Chanchal Dey

# Acknowledgements

We offer our sincere thanks to Prof. (Dr.) Ranjan Chakrabarti, Hon'ble Vice Chancellor of Vidyasagar University, Midnapore for his constant encouragement to complete our work.

We are indebted to Prof. (Dr.) R. P. Banerjee, Chairman & Director, EIILM-Kolkata for providing the invaluable guidance to our work.

We thank all the research scholars and teachers of Department of Business Administration, Vidyasagar University, Midnapore and Department of Humanities, CEM Kolaghat for their advice and suggestions.

We owe a lot to the authorities of Vidyasagar University and CEM Kolaghat for providing the necessary support.

Dr. Debasish Biswas
Chanchal Dey

# Abbreviations

| | |
|---|---|
| AIC | Atal Incubation Centres |
| AIM | Atal Innovation Mission |
| ANOVA | Analysis of Variance |
| ASEAN | The Association of Southeast Asian Nations |
| ATL | Atal Tinkering Laboratories |
| BIRAC | Biotechnology Industry Research Assistance Council |
| CEO | Chief Executive Officer |
| CHW | Community Health Worker |
| CII | Confederation of Indian Industry |
| COB | Carry on Business |
| EDII | Entrepreneurship Development Institute of India |
| EIA | Environmental Impact Assessment |
| EPF | Employees' Provident Fund |
| ESI | Employees' State Insurance |
| ICC | Internal Complaints Committee |
| IFCI | Industrial Finance Corporation of India |
| ICICI | Industrial Credit and Investment Corporation of India |
| IDBI | Industrial Development Bank of India |
| IPR | Intellectual Property Rights |
| ISO | International Organisation of Standardisation |
| IRR | Internal Rate of Return |
| IT | Information Technology |
| KVIC | Khadi and Village Industries Commission |
| LLP | Limited Liability Partnership |
| LNTECC | Larsen and Toubro Engineering and Construction Company |
| MCA | Ministry of Corporate Affairs |
| MD | Managing Director |
| MFI | Micro Finance Institutions |
| MIT | Massachusetts Institute of Technology |
| MSDE | Ministry of Skill Development & Entrepreneurship |

| | |
|---|---|
| MSE | Micro and Small Enterprises |
| MSME | Micro, Small and Medium Enterprises |
| NASSCOM | National Association of Software and Service Companies |
| NIDC | National Industrial Development Corporation |
| NGO | Non-Governmental Organisation |
| NPV | Net Present Value |
| NSIC | National Small Industries Corporation |
| NRDC | National Research Development Corporation |
| PHC | Primary Health Centres |
| PI | Profitability Index |
| PNB | Punjab National Bank |
| R&D | Research and Development |
| SBI | State Bank of India |
| SC | Scheduled Caste |
| SIDBI | Small Industries Development Bank of India |
| SEZ | Special Economic Zone |
| SFC | State Finance Corporation |
| SIDC | State Industries Development Corporation |
| SIDO | Small Industries Development Organisation |
| SME | Small- and Medium-Sized Enterprise |
| SMGULP | Sri Mahila Griha Udyog Lijjat Papad |
| SSI | Small-Scale Industries |
| SSIDC | State Small Industries Development Corporation |
| ST | Scheduled Tribes |
| S&T | Science and Technology |
| STEM | Science, Technology, Engineering, and Math |
| TPV | Total Present Value |
| WHIMS | Wireless Health Incident Monitoring System |
| XLRI | Xavier Labour Relations Institute |
| ₹ | Indian Rupee |

# About the Authors

**Dr. Debasish Biswas** is presently serving as an Assistant Professor and Head in the Department of Business Administration, Vidyasagar University, West Bengal. He joined Vidyasagar University on 2 April 2012. He was awarded M.Phil. in Commerce from Periyar University in 2008 and Ph.D. in commerce on 7 September 2011 by University of North Bengal. His area of research was 'Productivity & Industrial Relations'. Dr. Biswas obtained M.Com. in 2000 and MBA (HR) in 2002 from Burdwan University. He obtained Diploma in Labour Laws in 2003 and Post Graduate Diploma in Hospital Management in 2006 from Annamalai University. He also obtained Post Graduate Diploma in Marketing Management, Post Graduate Diploma in Entrepreneurship, and Post Graduate Diploma in Financial Management from Annamalai University in 2015, 2016, and 2017, respectively. Dr. Biswas qualified NET in Human Resource in 2008. He has post-graduate teaching experience of more than nine years. His areas of specialisations are Accounting & Finance, Human Resource, and Marketing. Dr. Biswas is a prolific researcher. He has presented 87 research papers in different areas of management in different National and International Seminars and Conferences. He has authored 64 research papers in National and International journals of repute. He acted as a resource person in different National and International Seminars in different parts of India. He is a life member of Indian Commerce Association and All India Accounting Association. He has authored 15 books titled: (1) Management Information System, (2) Fundamentals of Financial Management, (3) Industrial Relations & Labour Welfare, (4) The Romance of Human Resource Management, (5) Relationship between Productivity and Industrial Relations, (6) Compensation Management, (7) Human Resource Management for UGC NET, (8) Dynamic Evolution of Management Paradigm (Edited Bok), (9) Research Methodology for Social Sciences, (10) Human Capital Components and Customer Satisfaction in Hotel Industry, (11) Agribusiness Management,

(12) Agricultural Marketing, (13) Employee Performance: An Analytical Study with Reference to Public Power Generating Organisations in West Bengal, (14) Management-UGC NET, and (15) Financial Statement Analysis. He has also contributed 14 chapters in various edited books. He received Best Business Academic of the Year Award-2016 (Gold Medal) at the 69th All India Commerce Conference organised by Lucknow University, Lucknow. He has received Bharat Vikas Award in 2018 by Institute of Self Reliance, Odisha. Dr. Biswas developed study materials of MBA course for the Distance Education wing of Tezpur Central University, Assam and also developed study materials of M. Com. course for the Distance Education wing of Vidyasagar University, West Bengal. He has successfully guided 09 Ph.D. scholars. He is an editorial board member of AR Research Publication (UGC Listed Journal).

**Chanchal Dey** is presently serving as an Assistant Professor in the Department of Humanities, College of Engineering and Management, Kolaghat, West Bengal. He has completed his B.E. from RTM Nagpur University in the year 2014. He has obtained his MBA from Vidyasagar University in 2017 and was also awarded University Gold Medal in the same year.

# 1 Introduction to Entrepreneurship

Entrepreneurship is associated with the creation of something that is new and scalable with the help of time and effort. Entrepreneurship is considered challenging and accompanies significant financial, social, and mental strain but it is also equally rewarding. Psychological, social, personal, environmental, and economic factors have profound effects on entrepreneurship development.

## 1.1 Meaning

*Entrepreneurship*

Entrepreneurship refers to the art of creating, nurturing, and sustaining a business unit with the intention of generating profits in the future. Through entrepreneurship, an entrepreneur looks to take action towards bringing a positive change in society alongside bringing people together. Entrepreneurs transform and execute their ideas into action. Entrepreneurship is the collection of skills of an entrepreneur including the tendency to take risks and aspirations to build wealth.

According to Hisrich (1988), entrepreneurship is a dynamic process dedicated to the creation of wealth. It refers to doing something new by devoting time, effort, and undertaking the financial, emotional, social, and psychological risks. In return, entrepreneurship gives both monetary and non-monetary benefits in the form of personal satisfaction and freedom to the individual.

Kuratko and Hodgetts (2004) opined that entrepreneurship is a process that involves creation and innovation by four elements, that is, individual, organisation, environment, and cooperation with the agencies in Government, institutes.

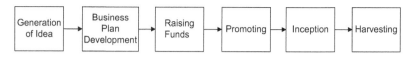

*Figure 1.1* Entrepreneurial process

## Characteristics of Entrepreneurship

- *Perpetual process*: Entrepreneurship is a creative, structured, and enduring process for managing the business efficiently.
- *Innovation* is the essential characteristic of entrepreneurship that brings a change in the market and helps the enterprise to be positioned favourably.
- *Measuring risks*: An entrepreneurial venture in order to survive must be able to identify the risks involved. Although calculated risks are taken to generate profits but only after due consideration.
- *Making profits* is one of the strongest impulses in entrepreneurship. It helps in smooth operation which leads to the expansion of the business.
- *Network building*: Entrepreneurship helps in building strong networks with suppliers, distributors, banks, and other stakeholders which helps to operate the business smoothly.
- *Market trends*: In order to stay competitive, entrepreneurial ventures must assess market trends periodically. This also enables to be ready for future uncertainties in the market.

### *Entrepreneur*

An entrepreneur is an individual who satisfies a specific need of the society with his/her pioneering idea. Entrepreneurs make a modern business successful as they spot opportunities, lay innovation that brings profits, and helps the business remain competitive. Some of the important qualities of an entrepreneur are to be innovative, optimistic, independent, team player, perseverant, committed, and so on.

According to Scarborough and Zimmerer (1988), an entrepreneur creates new business and faces uncertain circumstances to obtain profit and growth by identifying opportunities and come up with means to accomplish the same. Kuratko and Hodgetts (2004) opined that an entrepreneur is the one who tries to organise, manage, and bear the risks in business. Entrepreneurs with their dedication and commitment obtain new resources and revive the existing ones to generate profit. Some famous names such as Steve Jobs, Bill Gates, Larry Page, Jeff Bezos, Mark Zuckerberg, and many more have changed the world with their innovative and unique products and services.

*Table 1.1* Difference between entrepreneur and entrepreneurship

| Sl. no. | Entrepreneur | Entrepreneurship |
|---|---|---|
| 1. | An entrepreneur is an individual who has an innovative idea and works to transform it into reality alongside enduring the risks involved | Entrepreneurship refers to the activity of initiating a business, usually a start-up that offers unique products and services to the customers |
| 2. | It indicates an individual with a unique idea and wishes to realise it | It is a procedure that takes steps to make the idea happen |
| 3. | The individual pursues an innovative idea until it fructifies | It is the process by which an innovation is implemented |

*Table 1.2* Difference between entrepreneur and enterprise

| Sl. no. | Entrepreneur | Enterprise |
|---|---|---|
| 1. | It refers to an individual | It refers to the business entity |
| 2. | The individual takes the risk | It is the unit that involves risk and uncertainty |
| 3. | The individual makes the decision | It acts as the blueprint where decisions regarding the products and services are taken and implemented |
| 4. | The individual himself/herself indulged in the production and distribution of the offerings | It signifies the harmony between the staff and production as well as the distribution of the offerings |

*Table 1.3* Difference between entrepreneur and intrapreneur

| Sl. no. | Entrepreneur | Intrapreneur |
|---|---|---|
| 1. | The individual who establishes his/her own business with an innovative concept | The employee of an organisation responsible for bringing innovations in the products and services of the organisation |
| 2. | Relies on instincts | Responsible for the revival of offerings |
| 3. | Utilises the resources of his/her own | Organisation provides the resources |
| 4. | Responsible for raising his/her own capital | Organisation provides the required finance |
| 5. | Establishes a new enterprise | Works in the existing organisation |
| 6. | Works independently | Work depends on the organisational guidelines |
| 7. | Risks are undertaken by the individual | Risks are borne by the organisation |

*Table 1.4* Difference between entrepreneur and manager

| Sl. no. | Entrepreneur | Manager |
|---|---|---|
| 1. | An individual who builds an enterprise and bears the risks involved with the motive of making profits | An individual who is responsible for managing and administering an organisation |
| 2. | The intention is to bring innovation to the market | The intention is to get more authority or maintain the status quo |
| 3. | Works as an owner | Works as an employee |
| 4. | Mostly focused on start-ups | It is focused on the existing operations |
| 5. | Works in an informal setup | Works in a formal setup |
| 6. | Generally, takes risks | Generally, avoids risks |
| 7. | Take decisions based on instincts | Take decisions based on the facts and contingencies |

## 1.2   Background

Marco Polo is often regarded as one of the first entrepreneurs in the world. In the middle ages, an entrepreneur referred to people who controlled large production projects. In some cases, entrepreneurs could also control the projects where resources are supplied by the Government. Entrepreneurs also happen to be priests who had the authority to construct public buildings, churches, and so on.

During the 17th century, an entrepreneur was the individual who entered into a contract with the Government for the supply of agreed services or goods under fixed terms and prices. All the profits, losses, and risks involved were borne by the entrepreneurs. A French-Irish economist, Richard Cantillon remarked entrepreneurs were like insurance against risks (Nevin, 2013). John Law of France was one of the famous entrepreneurs of his time who founded The Royal Bank of France (Murphy, 1997).

In the 18th century, with rapid industrialisation, an entrepreneur referred to someone who seeks capital to fund his/her innovative pursuits. Thomas Edison who invented and developed a lot of innovative technologies was seen to be a capital user rather than a provider as he was unable to fund himself (Israel, 1998). A French economist Jean-Baptiste Say is credited to coin the term 'entrepreneur' around 1800 (Carlen, 2016). He opined that entrepreneurs move economic resources from lower to higher areas of productivity for greater yield (Koolman, 1971).

The role of entrepreneurs evolved a lot during the 19th century. An entrepreneur was someone who has started a business from scratch and was involved in each aspect of business functions in the early stages. Andrew

Carnegie, who hailed from an impoverished Scottish family, made American Steel Industry to be one of the strongest forces to reckon with (Nasaw, 2007).

In the 20th century, entrepreneurs were started to be seen as someone capable of disrupting the existing norms by introducing innovation and novel ideas. American banker J.P. Morgan revolutionised the American banking industry with his vision and revamped the economy of the US (Carosso, 1987).

In the 21st century, entrepreneurs are admired as heroes and role models. This century has been shaped by technological wonders. Today, the development and progress of start-ups are seen as parameters for economic growth. Entrepreneurs have made things affordable, and the quality of lives of average people has improved. Entrepreneurship has found a regular place in the education curriculum. Even the society tries to instil the entrepreneurial spirit among its young members.

## 1.3 Importance

An entrepreneur is an individual who sees an opportunity in the problem. The solutions which they develop are focused to improve society. We will discuss what makes entrepreneurs so important to society.

- *Entrepreneurs contribute to economic development* by creating employment opportunities and developing new markets that add to the national income.
- *Entrepreneurs bring change to society*: Entrepreneurs aim to explore and create something that has the potential to change the world. They aim to improve the world through their products and services.
- *Entrepreneurs give back to society*: Entrepreneurs pay regular taxes that help to fund social causes. Entrepreneurs have become involved in charities that help poor communities to access facilities such as drinking water and health care.

We will discuss some of the common reasons that motivate people to become entrepreneurs.

- *To bring change*: As entrepreneurs aim to bring change for better. They build enterprises which strive for exploration that have not been done before such as building electric vehicles, solar-based electricity, utilisation of renewable resources, and so forth. They want their innovations to reach common people and make their life better. Entrepreneurs love to experiment, learn, and work for sustained growth.
- *To secure livelihood*: Some individuals take up entrepreneurship by compulsion. It is also seen as a source of employment. It can give them freedom from workplace uncertainties and office politics. Hence, it acts

as an alternative career option for these individuals who fail to secure a job, for some or the other reason.

- *To be their own boss*: Entrepreneurs often feel repressed and choked when they work under someone. They feel their potential is not being utilised to full potential and are restricted to do something new. They want to have creative freedom and work according to their own terms. In other words, they don't fit into work in a corporate setup.

- *To work in a flexible manner*: Entrepreneurship allows people to work flexibly and with comparatively fewer strings attached. Entrepreneurs can work when they want to as they are their own boss. Moreover, entrepreneurship does not compel to work in a specific location as long as it is productive. One can work from home or any place based on his/her preference.

- *To take risks and challenges*: Entrepreneurs like to work on challenging problems that involve considerable risks too. Entrepreneurship is dedicated to innovation which also bear risks and challenges to develop solutions to create a difference. This sets them apart from others. They are ambitious, hardworking, and work along the path of challenges to become successful.

## 1.4    Factors That Influence Entrepreneurship

Entrepreneurship is influenced by a number of economic, social, political, psychological, and other factors. The positive influences present a conducive atmosphere for the practice of entrepreneurship, and negative influences are detrimental for entrepreneurship to prosper. We will discuss some of these factors here.

### 1.4.1    Personal Factors

The following characteristics of an individual make one successful entrepreneur:

- To take lead and come up with new ideas (Initiator)
- To take calculated risks with detailed analysis (Risk-taker)
- To work tirelessly towards achieving goals along with the obstacles (Perseverant)
- To convince others about new concepts and ideas (Persuasive)
- To be able to hunt and take advantage of opportunities (Proactive)

We have discussed these characteristics and competencies of an entrepreneur in detail in the next chapter.

### *1.4.2 Psychological Factors*

Psychological factors are important in the case of entrepreneurship in the following ways:

- *Achieving needs*: The motivation for achieving needs and cultural factors help entrepreneurs to be successful. This makes entrepreneurs take risks and work hard to achieve their goals. The role of societies alongside parental influence is considered important.
- *Loss of status*: It is seen that in case a group loses status and power, it instigates the group members to take up entrepreneurship to make money and climb the social ladder. Entrepreneurship helps to regain lost prestige in such cases.
- *Other motives* for entrepreneurs include recognition, self-esteem, wealth, power, security, and to do service to society. Entrepreneurs also love to develop solutions for challenging problems and are not afraid of taking risks. Entrepreneurship helps them to work independently and be their own boss.

### *1.4.3 Social Factors*

Social factors also have a crucial role in shaping entrepreneurial behaviour, which results in the growth of entrepreneurship. Some of these major factors are as follows:

- *Background*: The composition and economic status of the family also affect entrepreneurial behaviour. The occupation, background, and social status of the family give added mileage when it comes to entrepreneurship.
- *Education system*: It is also important for instilling the entrepreneurial spirit in an individual. Entrepreneurship has been given importance and has already made it to the curriculum. Education makes one find meaningful solutions to solve societal problems through innovation as it also develops intellectual aptitude.
- *Culture*: A culture that recognises entrepreneurs are the competitive ones. It provokes men to work for excellence. It makes people ambitious and relentless in their pursuits to attain success, recognition, and social status through entrepreneurial activities.
- *Society*: It influences entrepreneurial behaviour to a great extent. Societies with a positive attitude towards entrepreneurship attain progress through innovation and new ideas.
- *Caste*: The value system of a society that has evolved over a long time influences the activities of people. Let's consider the caste system practiced

among Hindus where the society is divided into four castes, that is, The *Brahmana* (priest), the *Kshatriya* (warrior), the *Vaishya* (trade), and the *Shudra* (artisan). For a long time, commercial activities were under the dominance of the *Vaishya* community as the other three *varnas* were not interested in the same (Gupta, 2000). This is similar in other parts of the world too, where certain ethnic groups have a higher presence in entrepreneurial activities.

### 1.4.4    Economic Factors

Economic factors have a considerable influence on the success of entrepreneurship in the following ways:

*   *Market* decides the survival of a business. For a venture to be successful, the quality of the offerings should be high and affordable at the same time. This will help in the favourable positioning of the enterprise in the market and will bring a competitive advantage.
*   *Capital* is regarded as a key element for setting up an enterprise. Higher capital investments in feasible projects result in greater profits and help the entrepreneurship to prosper. Adequate funding helps the enterprise to compete in the market, bring innovation to the offerings, and makes it sustainable.
*   *Raw materials* or production inputs are the precursors in any enterprise. Entrepreneurs must ensure there is an uninterrupted supply of inputs, so that the consistency and quality of production are not hit. There should be proper mechanisms at the place to map the status of existing raw materials or inputs in the enterprise.
*   *Labour* is essential for the quality and price of the offerings of the enterprise. Skilled manpower ensures better productivity and sustainability to the enterprise. The availability of low-cost labour with flexible mobility is something greatly preferred by entrepreneurs.
*   *Infrastructure*: Adequate network connectivity and transportation amenities are essential for the progress of entrepreneurship. The facilities such as drainage, electricity, and water encourages an entrepreneur to start a business.

### 1.4.5    Environmental Factors

Environmental factors refer to the conditions in which an entrepreneur works. These factors have a substantial influence on entrepreneurship. We have discussed some of the important environmental factors here.

*   *Politics*: The subsidies, schemes, policies, and support provided by the Government go a long way to decide regarding the setting up an enterprise.

- *Legislation*: Various legal formalities and labour laws are important to determine the establishment of a business.
- *Economy*: The state of the economy determines demand and supply. This leads to deciding the scale of investment for the business.
- *Finance*: The availability of funding options, funding sources, and related policies have a great influence on entrepreneurship.
- *Society and culture*: It determines the nature, type, and extent of the products and services offered. It should comply with the tastes and preferences of the target population.

## 1.5 Factors Responsible for Entrepreneurship Growth

There are certain indicators that give a positive outlook on the growth of entrepreneurship (Tur-Porcar et al., 2018). We have discussed some of these factors here.

- *Optimum utilisation of resources*: The adequate presence of the required business inputs, that is, raw materials, manpower, electricity, and so on, is conducive for entrepreneurship growth. It results in the efficient management and utilisation of resources with minimum losses.
- *Returns*: The return on investment which is measured by net profits, sales revenue, and so forth helps to determine the financial health of an organisation. Good returns will be encouraging to the growth of entrepreneurship.
- *Business expansion*: The good returns will promote entrepreneurs to expand their enterprise by increasing the production capacity and employing more employees. This may even lead to diversification and new products can be introduced. It is a win-win situation for both entrepreneurs as well as consumers.
- *Gestation period*: It is the time gap of the date between incorporation and commencement of operations. The longer gestation period is unfavourable for entrepreneurship as the project gets delayed and will take a longer time to reach break-even. Factors such as difficulty in raising funds, red tape, unavailability of manpower, raw materials, plant, and machinery make the gestation period longer.
- *Role of government*: Government strategies, policies, and schemes should support the entrepreneurship ecosystem. This will create employment opportunities, increase imports, cultivate research and development, and so on. Ultimately, all these will lead to economic development. In India, various organisations have been established in order to promote entrepreneurship development such as National Small Industries Corporation (NSIC) Limited, Khadi and Village Industries Commission (KVIC), National Bank for Agriculture and Rural Development, State Industries Development Corporation, and so forth.

We have specifically discussed the different organisations working for entrepreneurship development in Chapter 6.

## References

Carlen, J. (2016). *A brief history of entrepreneurship: The pioneers, profiteers, and racketeers who shaped our world.* New York & Chichester, West Sussex: Columbia University Press.

Carosso, V. P. (1987). *The Morgans: Private international bankers, 1854–1913.* Cambridge, MA: Harvard University Press.

Gupta, D. (2000). *Interrogating caste: Understanding hierarchy and difference in Indian society.* New Delhi: Penguin Books.

Hisrich, R. D. (1988). Entrepreneurship: Past, present, and future. *Journal of Small Business Management, 26*(4), 1.

Israel, P. (1998). *Edison: A life of invention.* New York: John Wiley.

Koolman, G. (1971). Say's conception of the role of the entrepreneur. *Economica, 38*(151), new series, 269–286.

Kuratko, D. F., & Hodgetts, R. M. (2004). *Entrepreneurship: Theory, process, practice.* Mason, OH: South-Western College Publishers.

Murphy, A. E. (1997). *John Law: Economic theorist and policy-market.* Oxford: Clarendon Press.

Nasaw, D. (2007). *Andrew Carnegie.* New York: Penguin Books.

Nevin, S. (2013). Richard Cantillon: The father of economics. *History Ireland, 21*(2), 20–23.

Scarborough, N. M., & Zimmerer, T. W. (1988). The entrepreneur's guide to ESOPs. *Compensation & Benefits Review, 20*(4), 62–68.

Tur-Porcar, A., Roig-Tierno, N., & Llorca Mestre, A. (2018). Factors affecting entrepreneurship and business sustainability. *Sustainability, 10*(2), 452.

# 2 Entrepreneurship Around Us

Entrepreneurial culture plays a crucial role in shaping the entrepreneurial spirit and motivation to become an entrepreneur. The culture makes society prosperous. An entrepreneur should have the necessary skills, abilities, and knowledge to be competent and successful in business (Brownson, 2013). With an increasing population of educated youth and shrinking job opportunities, entrepreneurship has the potential of bringing a new revolution in the country.

## 2.1 Entrepreneurial Culture

We will understand the two distinct words which form the term 'Entrepreneurial Culture'. 'Entrepreneurial' refers to the specific style of the entrepreneur to achieve his objectives. 'Culture' implies the way of life, beliefs, attributes, and so on, which are conveyed across generations. Therefore, the significance of entrepreneurial culture on business can be clearly understood.

Kundu (2009) has classified the entrepreneurial culture in three levels as follows:

**First level:** This level is invisible and unconscious at the same time. This level takes only the attributes and values into consideration. Attributes act as the natural indicators which help in understanding the likelihood of a person to become an entrepreneur. These attributes encourage an individual to pursue entrepreneurship. The decision-making and the behaviour of an entrepreneur depends on his value system, which help him to make a clear distinction between right and wrong. The values such as taking initiative, being innovative, able to take risks, competitive, and so forth can be linked to entrepreneurship.

**Second level:** This level is either semi-visible or semi-conscious, there is a presence of entrepreneurial mindset. The entrepreneurial mindset refers to the attitude which orients the response of an entrepreneur towards a certain occurrence by virtue of a learned predisposition. The attitudes provide the foundation to human behaviour which motivates and inculcates the feeling of personal accomplishment. The entrepreneurial attitudes influence and also get influenced by the past experiences of the individual and how one thinks and feels about what he went through.

Many studies have shown, participation in well-designed entrepreneurial programmes enriches the entrepreneurial culture among the attendees.

**Third level:** This level is visible and shows entrepreneurial behaviour. This entrepreneurial behaviour results in the initiation of business by the individual.

As per Williams-Middleton (2010), entrepreneurial behaviour is basically a set of actions which undergoes a continuous alteration until the positioning and acceptance of the defined opportunity. This finally results in the creation of a new business.

## 2.2  Entrepreneurial Society

Ojomo (2016) gave the following features are unique for an entrepreneurial society:

* *Innovation should always come before regulation*: Innovation is an important characteristic of an entrepreneurial society. Bangalore is the place where most of the technological innovations take place in India. These innovations which are directed towards the improvement of lives by creating viable solutions must ensure that they are at least one step ahead of regulators. However, in case of regulations precede innovation, it will be discouraging for the entrepreneurial psyche of the innovators (Drucker, 1985).
* *The advent of modularised work*: The idea of work and the work itself becomes modularised in an entrepreneurial society. The work is becoming project-specific and resulting in short-term engagements as opposed to the traditional concept of long-term employment contracts and eight-hour shift rule. The new-age start-ups such as Ola, Swiggy, Big Basket, and so on, which connect the demand and supply of labour, indicate that societies are becoming more entrepreneurial these days.
* *The accomplishments of innovators and entrepreneurs must get recognition*: Entrepreneurs are recognised, appreciated, and make a profit through their work in a society that is based on entrepreneurial culture. They are considered successful and looked upon as role models in society. However, in a non-entrepreneurial society, bureaucrats

and politicians are the most financially rewarded people as they act as decision and policymakers. This becomes a hurdle to the free-thinking mindset of the innovators and entrepreneurs (Drucker, 1985). Today, start-ups and entrepreneurship have become a rage in India and are becoming a popular career option among the youth.

• *Either the society is prosperous or is approaching prosperity*: Growth and prosperity are different. In the 2000s, some countries in Africa such as Nigeria, Equatorial Guinea, Angola, and so forth were some of the fastest-growing economies but could not create prosperity for millions of its citizens. The living standards and the income levels remained unchanged for the poor according to the research carried out by Pew Research Center. This was in direct contrast if we study the growth which took place in the Asian economies like South Korea during the 1950s and 1960s, where the private sector was nurtured and encouraged in the form of Samsung, LG, and Hyundai. After the liberalisation of Indian economy in 1991, the economy has witnessed tremendous growth, but it has not resulted in the uniform or collective prosperity of the citizens (Mohan, 2018).

• *The dependency of Government on the creativity of innovators*: Innovations that are geared towards solving societal issues ensure long-term growth and prosperity. To remain competitive, relevant, and vibrant, the government must encourage entrepreneurship and innovation. However, when Governments rely mostly on natural resources for economic prosperity and growth, it can become vulnerable to commodity prices in the international markets.

Innovation and entrepreneurship are the key drivers of an entrepreneurial society, where people have a choice of what they do and when they do it.

## 2.3 Entrepreneurial Potential in a Prospective Entrepreneur

A business owner has to put up a lot of hard work and also be ready for the stress associated to be successful. A successful entrepreneur has to be determined and courageous to come up with a unique idea and then transform that very idea into action. As per a joint study conducted by IBM Institute for Business Value and Oxford Economics, 90 percent of Indian start-ups don't go beyond the first five years (Mehrotra et. al., 2016). Hence, the notion of quitting a well-paid job and becoming an entrepreneur is debated in Indian context.

For an entrepreneur, this risk seems a reward for those who know the time and efforts to be put in to transform their dream into reality. The ideal combination of the right attitude and personality is very important for the success of an entrepreneur. Miller (2020) suggested ten essential character-istics to be successful entrepreneurs are as follows:

- **Creative**

  The success of entrepreneurship depends on coming up with new ideas that have the potential to better the present way of doing things. Entre-preneurs think outside the box, come up with innovative solutions, and are simply not satisfied with the existing state. Earning money is not the sole concern of a successful entrepreneur rather solve an existing issue in the best way possible.

- **Optimistic**

  Entrepreneurs always look for the positive side and are full of imagina-tion. They hunt for new ways which can better the existing way of our life. They are never stuck in the past and are focused on the new pos-sibilities. An entrepreneur sees a problem as an opportunity that encour-ages them to do better things.

- **Motivated**

  Due to the motivation of doing things differently and strong ideas makes an entrepreneur put long working hours to run a new business successfully. As the entrepreneur is his/her own boss, one should have the passion to work with strong initiative. Perseverance acts as the cata-lyst in the making of a successful entrepreneur.

- **Passionate**

  Passion ensures long-term success and gives the much-needed purpose to an entrepreneur. It helps an entrepreneur to develop a relentless atti-tude and dedication which makes them confident about the way things are done by them in the business.

- **Resourceful**

  A successful entrepreneur proceeds with a plan and has a clearly defined purpose. Every resource such as time, money, and efforts are to be utilised systematically. Entrepreneurs should always be ready for the upcoming challenges and ensure the existing resources are utilised optimally. They value existing resources and always like to keep them in their best version.

- **Future-oriented**

  As entrepreneurs are driven towards the future, they are goal-oriented which are realistic and practical. The setting of a goal propels them to success and develops a strong vision. This makes them proactive and helps them to anticipate the things beforehand.

- **Flexible**

  Most entrepreneurs start their journey solo with limited staff and resources. To become successful, one should always be open to learn new skills. This will help in adjusting to the demands and circumstances. They tend to approach things with a broad mind and are mindful of the various possibilities. The rigidity and inability to adapt should be averted for successful entrepreneurs.

- **Persuasive**

  A successful entrepreneur must be a self-believer who can easily get along with others to make them listen to his/her ideas. At times, people take time to accept a radical idea. However, people will generally be sceptical to invest and provide support for an out-of-the-box idea. A successful entrepreneur must be persuasive about their ideas and convince others about the same.

- **Decisive**

  One cannot employ delaying tactics in business. The importance of decision-making by entrepreneurs looms large in defining the success of the business. They have to be prompt, adaptive, and quick to make the maximum of opportunities. A successful entrepreneur simply cannot let go of a rewarding opportunity because of time-lapse.

- **Adventurous**

  A successful entrepreneur takes judicious and calculative risks. But these risks are deeply analysed before decision-making. They are proactive about their plans and even these risks are only taken if it has the potential to make their existing business better.

## 2.4   Entrepreneurial Skills and Competencies

A successful entrepreneur has certain traits that make him/her different from others. The competency of an entrepreneur refers to the calibre required to run a business effectively and efficiently. According to Boyatzis (1982), competency is the underlying feature of a person which causes superior or effective performance at work.

Competency consists of unique and broad knowledge, skills, abilities, motives, and so on that are instilled in an individual. These competencies can be inherited or are developed in the way of learning and experience. Entrepreneurial competencies refer to the conscious or subconscious use of such traits which results in higher performance when it comes to entrepreneurial activities.

### 2.4.1   Major Entrepreneurial Competencies

Unlike in the past, today it is accepted that entrepreneurs are made, not born. The entrepreneurial competencies determine whether the entrepreneur will be successful or not. These competencies are in the form of skills, abilities, and knowledge acquired through education and experience.

A joint research project based on India, Malawi, and other countries was carried out by Entrepreneurship Development Institute of India (EDII), Ahmedabad, and behavioural scientist David C. McClelland. The research identified some of the following competencies which ensure superior performance in carrying out entrepreneurial activities (Raval & Murali, 1987).

- *Initiative*: Entrepreneurs should always be ready to take the lead rather than delaying the proceedings.
- *Opportunity seeker*: Entrepreneurs seek opportunities and apply suitable action to seize the same.
- *Perseverance*: Entrepreneurs should not back down in the face of a difficult situation rather continue their efforts to reach the aim.
- *Informative*: Entrepreneur should seek relevant and accurate information through research, consultation, analysis, and so forth.
- *Quality of work*: Entrepreneurs work hard for the high quality of work to make a reputation of their own.
- *Commitment*: Entrepreneurs are dedicated towards meeting deadlines about their work.
- *Planning*: Entrepreneurs approach anything with realistic planning to complete the task.
- *Problem-solving*: Entrepreneurs are ever ready to find a way out of complicated situations.
- *Self-belief*: Entrepreneurs are confident and believe in getting things done efficiently.
- *Monitor*: Entrepreneurs monitor regular growth and devise ways to improve existing activities.
- *Concerned about employees*: Entrepreneurs care about their employees and ensure employee satisfaction.
- *Strategist*: Entrepreneurs implement innovative strategies for the smooth running of the business.

These entrepreneurial skills and competencies help an entrepreneur to perform better than rivals. Sharma (2005) proposed the following factors to measure Entrepreneurial Performance (EP), which is expressed as,

EP = f (SB, MF, KA, FS and EV)

- *Socio-cultural background (SB)* refers to the upbringing and family background of the entrepreneur which influences his/her values and attitudes.
- *Motivational force (MF)* indicates factors such as wealth, recognition, and so on, which inspires an individual to become an entrepreneur.
- *Knowledge and ability (KA)* refers to the educational qualification, skills, and experience of the entrepreneur.
- *Financial strength (FS)* refers to the amount of funds an entrepreneur can raise through internal and external sources.
- *Environmental variables (EV)* comprise the availability of manpower, raw material, market situation, and Government policies.

## 2.5   New Trends in Entrepreneurship Development

Entrepreneurship is becoming a trend nowadays. It reflects the readiness, risk-taking ability, and handling of business within a well-defined structure in this dynamic world. According to a Workmonitor survey conducted by Randstad (2017), 83 percent of respondents' harbour dreams of becoming an entrepreneur in India. Moreover, 86 percent of respondents feel India is a right place to run a start-up. The culture of building start-ups has become a source of enthusiasm for today's youth due to the advancement of knowledge and technology. Modern start-ups are confronting traditional companies with their innovative techniques. It works towards new thoughts and brings innovation to the existing thought process for quality improvement. These businesses are pretty straightforward and are consistently driven by the outcomes. Young entrepreneurs in India do not like to work in traditional workplaces rather they hunt for opportunities to apply their innovative ideas and turn these to reality. Start-ups give direction to these individuals who aim to transform their ideas into a scalable business. To create a sustainable entrepreneurship ecosystem, the Indian Government has also been encouraging steps by introducing loans, subsidies, schemes, and so forth for the new start-ups through youth entrepreneur programmes. This can be remarkable to India's progress towards becoming an entrepreneurial society. In the Randstad's Workmonitor survey, 84 percent of respondents opined that Indian Government actively supports start-ups in the country.

## 2.6    Economic Development Through Entrepreneurship

Economic development is indicated by the economic growth and increase of per capita income of a country across a period of time. We see that entrepreneurship plays a leading role in the economy of developed nations such as the US, Germany, Japan, and so on. The awareness about entrepreneurship and economy is somewhat less in the case of developing and under-developed nations. However, now the policymakers have started encouraging entrepreneurship development as they have realised the potential it offers for economic development in the countries with the available production factors in the form of land, labour, capital, and material (Toma et. al., 2014). The extent of this correlation varies across nations due to the available resources, technology, climate, people, and politics. Under favourable conditions, entrepreneurship flourishes.

- The challenges for an entrepreneur are significant in the case of developing or underdeveloped territories because of scarce funding options, skilled manpower, government policies, and so on.
- Unfavourable market conditions and financial issues make an entrepreneur apprehensive to launch a venture in such locations. The establishments of large-scale ventures can bring rapid economic development in these areas.
- India aspires for a decentralised industrial structure to minimise the regional imbalances of economic development.
- This will help in the creation of employment opportunities, improving living standards, and will raise the increase of people.

*Role of entrepreneurship in the economic development of India*

- **Inclusive development**

Entrepreneurship ventures when operated successfully can lead to the process of industrialisation. These ventures will generate demand for raw material, accessories, equipment, food, accommodation, transportation, and so forth. To satisfy the demands, many other ventures will also start functioning. This goes like a chain reaction and ultimately brings more industrial units to operate which results in the inclusive development of the economy of the area.

- **Promotion of exports**

With higher production, entrepreneurs are able to export their products and services overseas. This helps in the generation of foreign exchange which has a positive impact on economic development.

- **Higher living standards**

The entrepreneurial ventures bring the latest innovations and high-quality goods and services at affordable prices. The basic premise of entrepreneurship is built on providing meaningful solutions to the existing problems and making lives of people better. This allows people to avail high-quality products and services at lesser prices that also improve the living standards of people.

- **Economic growth**

Entrepreneurship development results in the movement of resources of capital and skill. It leads to the development of new products, services, and markets. This results in the growth of the gross domestic product of the economy and increases the per capita income of the citizens.

- **Creation and distribution of wealth**

Entrepreneurial activities promote the equitable distribution of income and wealth. It cultivates the entrepreneurship spirit among the people to make them self-employed through optimal utilisation of resources. Entrepreneurship is not restricted to specific geography, demography, or section of people rather it works for balanced development.

- **Employment generation**

Entrepreneurship creates both direct and indirect sources of employment opportunities. It is particularly helpful for a country with a large population in the working-age group. This has also resulted in the awareness about skill development among the youth.

All these above-mentioned factors have prompted the government to take the necessary steps to encourage entrepreneurship development in the country.

## References

Boyatzis, R. E. (1982). *The competent manager: A model for effective performance.* New York: John Wiley & Sons.

Brownson, C. D. (2013). Fostering entrepreneurial culture: A conceptualization. *European Journal of Business and Management, 5,* 146–154.

Drucker, P. F. (1985). *Innovation and entrepreneurship: Practice and principles.* New York: Harper & Row.

Employment vs. Employability [Report]. (q1, 2017). Randstad Workmonitor.

Kundu, K. (2009). Influence of organizational culture on the institution building process of an organization. *CURIE, 2*, 48–57.

Mehrotra, N., Patrao, C., Marshall, A., Banda, M., & Singh, R. R. (2016). *Entrepreneurial India: How start-ups redefine India's economic growth* [Report]. IBM Institute for Business Value.

Miller, K. (2020, July 7). 10 characteristics of successful entrepreneurs. *HBS Online*. Retrieved August 24, 2020, from https://online.hbs.edu/blog/post/characteristics-of-successful-entrepreneurs

Mohan, R. (2018). *India transformed: Twenty-five years of economic reforms* (Illustrated ed.). Washington, DC: Brookings Institution Press.

Ojomo, E. (2016, October 04). *6 signs you're living in an entrepreneurial society.* Retrieved July 24, 2020, from https://hbr.org/2016/10/6-signs-youre-living-in-an-entrepreneurial-society

Raval, H. C., & Murali, B. P. (1987). *Identification of entrepreneurial competencies and evolving tools and techniques for assessing the same.* EDI Ahmedabad Working Papers, WP-100.

Sharma, S., Singh, B., & Singhal, S. (2005). *Entrepreneurship development.* New Delhi: Wisdom Publications.

Toma, S., Grigore, A., & Marinescu, P. (2014). Economic development and entrepreneurship. *Procedia Economics and Finance, 8*, 436–443.

Williams Middleton, K. (2010). *Developing entrepreneurial behaviour: Facilitating nascent entrepreneurship at the university* [Published doctoral dissertation]. Chalmers University of Technology.

# 3 Classification
## Entrepreneurs and Entrepreneurship

Entrepreneurs are classified on the basis of various parameters such as demography, scale, ownership, motivation, and so on. We will also discuss various types of entrepreneurship. Entrepreneurship plays a significant role in raising the living standards of the society by solving social issues alongside making the lives of people better. Moreover, it has also been instrumental in the cause of women empowerment.

## 3.1 Danhof's Classification

Danhof (1949) classified entrepreneurs on the following four types:

- *Innovative entrepreneurs* are audacious to lead the novel ideas into reality. They are the ones who like to disrupt a market by bringing new products and services. These modern entrepreneurs vouch for innovation and invention. Most of them reside in developed countries where significant funding is available for research and development.
- *Imitative entrepreneurs* are those who are quick to adopt the successful innovations made by innovative entrepreneurs. These entrepreneurs are mostly seen in developing countries who make relevant modifications before imitating the innovations in the form of technologies and methods.
- *Fabian entrepreneurs* are somewhat prudent when it comes to trying out a different strategy in the business. These entrepreneurs are sluggish and respond to innovation only when there is no way out or to suffer losses. These entrepreneurs are confined to traditional styles and do not prefer to adapt to new changes.
- *Drone entrepreneurs* are identified as rigid and conventional who discard new techniques in spite of lesser profits. Due to this, they often let go of useful opportunities and after a certain time are discarded out of the market.

## 3.2   General Classification of Entrepreneurs

Entrepreneurs can be classified based on ownership, demography, stages of development, business, motivation, growth, technology, and so on.

### 3.2.1   *Based on Demography*

- *Area*: Urban and Rural
- *Gender*: Male and Female
- *Age*: Young, Middle-aged, and Old

### 3.2.2   *Based on Scale*

- *Small business entrepreneurs* are in the entry level with limited funding and in most cases offer one or two products or services.
- *Medium business entrepreneurs* are around for some time with a market presence. They have somewhat defined offerings.
- *Large business entrepreneurs* have a steady flow of funds and have diversified product line and service offerings. They are well established and look for a higher market share.

### 3.2.3   *Based on Stages of Development*

- *First-generation entrepreneurs* are from non-entrepreneurial backgrounds and establish their enterprise by embracing innovative ideas. The entrepreneur is the first in the family to establish an enterprise on his/her own. Those with a business background but establishing a completely unrelated business also come under this category.
- *Second-generation entrepreneurs* inherit the family business. However, in order to stay competitive, they adapt and improvise to the changing market needs.
- *Classical entrepreneurs* give more importance to business survival than growth. They are called stereotype entrepreneurs as they seek consistent returns with or without growth.
- *Inherited entrepreneurs* inherit family business alongside experience to run the family business. These entrepreneurs do not prefer much diversification or bringing a new approach to their family business.

### 3.2.4   *Based on Capital Ownership*

- *Private entrepreneur*: Entrepreneurial venture established by an individual or a group of individuals with the intent of making profits. The responsibilities of arranging finance and bearing the risks reside with the members.

- *State entrepreneur*: Entrepreneurial venture handled by state or the government itself.
- *Joint entrepreneur*: Entrepreneurial venture managed by both private and state entities.

### 3.2.5 Based on Growth

- *Growth entrepreneurs* prefer working in high growth ventures with continuous progress.
- *Super-growth entrepreneurs* show high performance in their venture measured by high profits and productivity.

Both growth and super-growth entrepreneurs look for making high profits and satisfaction at their work.

### 3.2.6 Based on Business Type

- *Business entrepreneurs* envisage novel ideas regarding a product or service and then transform it into reality. They also oversee the production and marketing aspects of both small and large business enterprises.
- *Trading entrepreneurs* are indulged in trading activities and not concerned with manufacturing activities. They are involved in the marketing and distribution of products and services.
- *Industrial entrepreneurs* refer to those who establish an industrial unit. They deal with industrial and production activities. They are involved in the manufacturing of products with the aim of satisfying the needs of consumers.
- *Corporate entrepreneurs* are responsible for planning, designing, and managing a corporate body. They are known for their innovative skills in leading and directing an organisation.
- *Agricultural entrepreneurs* are engaged in agricultural activities such as increasing agricultural output, organic farming, horticulture, and so on.
- *Retail entrepreneurs* take up trading activities that are customer-oriented and involve direct contact with customers.
- *Service entrepreneurs* offer different services to customers to make profits.
- *Social entrepreneurs* serve society and work on social issues without the motive of making profits.

### 3.2.7 Based on motivation

- *Pure entrepreneurs* may or may not have any competence for entrepreneurship. They are driven by the monetary rewards attached to a business venture. Factors such as status, recognition, wealth, and so forth motivate such entrepreneurs to start an entrepreneurial venture.

- *Induced entrepreneurs* are lured by the several schemes, incentives, subsidies, and so on given by the government to the entrepreneurs. The government assistance in the form of funding and technology motivates such people to start an entrepreneurial venture.
- *Motivated entrepreneurs* are driven by both economic factors and self-realisation. They have a genuine interest and want to become entrepreneurs to do something innovative which could disrupt the market.
- *Spontaneous entrepreneurs* have a natural flair to be an entrepreneur. They have self-belief and like to take up challenging entrepreneurial activities. They are resourceful and organised which makes them successful.

### 3.2.8    *Based on Technology*

- *Technical entrepreneurs* have a sound understanding of technology and are more concerned with the technical intricacies compared to the marketing aspects of the business. They work to bring innovation and invention in entrepreneurial ventures.
- *Non-technical entrepreneurs* are concerned with developing tactics for marketing and distribution of products and services to generate higher revenues.
- *Professional entrepreneurs* apply their innovative ideas to set up a business but are not interested in managing the same. Post establishment of the business, professional entrepreneurs sell it to someone else to operate.

## 3.3    Types of Entrepreneurship

We have studied various types of entrepreneurs; now, we will study some of the popular types of entrepreneurship ventures.

### 3.3.1    *Rural Entrepreneurship*

Mahatma Gandhi is credited with once saying 'India lives in its villages' (MIB, Govt. of India, 2000). Nearly 70 percent of the Indian population resides in rural areas where agriculture and related activities support livelihood. In order to solve rural-based issues such as unemployment and rapid migration to urban areas, industries in rural belts have to be developed. In other words, the development of the rural economy is a precursor to national development as well. This will significantly reduce the rural-urban differentials with regards to living standards.

Rural entrepreneurship can address the above concerns. Today, our rural sector has seen increasing connectivity and is also modernising at a fast pace. Hence, rural and tribal-based entrepreneurship can become an effective means to tackle issues of poverty, unemployment, and illiteracy as it will contribute to the process of rural development. Indian Government has attached tremendous importance and support to the growth and entrepreneurship in rural areas. The Government of India has formed a statutory body named KVIC formed in 1957 under a Parliamentary Act to encourage khadi and village industries in the rural belts of the country.

As per KVIC, the industry will be classified as a village industry:

- located in a rural area, producing goods or services with or without the use of power.
- fixed capital investment per worker will not be more than 1 lakh rupees. This can be modified by the Government from time to time through official notification.

Rural entrepreneurship refers to the establishment of business and industrial units in the rural sector of the economy. Rural entrepreneurship plays a significant role in bringing rural industrialisation at the grassroots level. Rural-based business and industrial units are generally agriculture-based. The village-based industries are of following types:

*Agro-based*, e.g., dairy products, jaggery, sugar, pickles, spices, fruit juices.
*Forest-based*, e.g., paper, gum, wood products, rubber, honey, bamboo products.
*Textile-based*, e.g., weaving, colouring, spinning, bleaching.

### 3.3.2   Agricultural Entrepreneurship

Agricultural entrepreneurship is focused on the management of agricultural inputs as well as agricultural products. Agricultural entrepreneurs aim to improve the quality of products, increase the yield, and sell it to the wider public. Organic farming, horticulture, and growing medicinal plants have increasingly been successful in attracting target customers. Moreover, farmers have also benefited as it helped them to increase profits and sales. The government also actively supports it under rural entrepreneurship.

### 3.3.3   Social Entrepreneurship

Social entrepreneurship is the practice of addressing social or environmental issues through innovative business methods. It has gained popularity across the world, where people from various sections of society are coming together to create and implement effective, innovative, and sustainable solutions against social and environmental challenges. These solutions are generally offered as goods and services which can be either profit or as a non-profit initiative.

Social entrepreneurship recognises social issues and implements the entrepreneurial principles to achieve a favourable transformation in society. It starts with research to define a specific social issue and then establishing a social enterprise to bring the desired transformation. The transformation doesn't always eliminate the issue completely and can be a lifelong process towards the improvement of the prevalent circumstances. Unlike business entrepreneurship, social entrepreneurship is focused on the development of social capital rather than monetary profit alone. Social entrepreneurs are mostly associated with non-profit organisations and non-government organisations. However, social entrepreneurs are also required to yield profits to sustain and to work towards bringing a desired revamp in the society. Social entrepreneurship mostly works on child rights, waste management, and women empowerment. It even looks for raising funds through charity, community proceedings, and so on. There are several remarkable social entrepreneurs who are recognised for their excellent work towards societal improvement.

The founder of Grameen Bank, Muhammad Yunus, is a Bangladesh-based social entrepreneur whose venture was to provide credit to poor entrepreneurs who are unable to secure traditional loans (Yunus & Jolis, 2003). He was a recipient of the prestigious Nobel Peace Prize in the year 2006.

Kailash Satyarthi is an Indian Nobel Laureate and social entrepreneur who worked for the eviction of child labour and universal access to education through his organisations such as Kailash Satyarthi Children's Foundation, Global Campaign for Education, and so forth (Satyarthi, 2020).

iKure, founded by Sujay Santra in 2010, a social venture aims to provide tech-based affordable primary healthcare which can be accessed by people even living in remote areas. As there is a dearth of competent doctors in village areas, iKure is revolutionising public healthcare by introducing a community-based healthcare system. Today, iKure is regarded as one of the pioneers in the development of the sustainable primary healthcare model in the world.

Under social entrepreneurship, these organisations address social issues and bring favourable societal changes. They work for social improvement and strive towards innovations that aim for bringing the necessary social change towards enhancement of the existing conditions in society. Social entrepreneurship has witnessed considerable growth and interest over the past few years. It has also been introduced in the university curriculum. It has helped those who wanted to contribute to the society and see a positive change in human lives. The Government has also encouraged social entrepreneurs as they can be instrumental to reach developmental goals.

### 3.3.4   Educational Entrepreneurship

Educational entrepreneurship is not a recent occurrence. Here, the entrepreneur identifies an issue in the education domain and develops solutions to address the same. In India, there are a lot of institutions that has flourished based on this. In recent years, young entrepreneurs have made huge in-roads in offering high quality and affordable educational services. These services range from offering admissions, coaching, conducting examinations, and so forth online. Many entrepreneurs have also established enterprises focusing on rural education and education for the marginal section of the population. Educational entrepreneurship has been booming in the country. Byjus, Vedantu, Unacademy, and so on have created a niche in educational entrepreneurship (Shanthi, 2020).

### 3.3.5   Women Entrepreneurship

Women entrepreneurship are those business enterprises where women think, initiate, organise, operate, and combine production inputs. They are also involved in undertaking the risks and handle the economic uncertainties associated with it (Startup India, 2020).

As per the Indian Government, under women entrepreneurship,

• an enterprise is owned and controlled by women
• women have the minimum financial interest of 51 percent of the capital
• women constitute at least 51 percent of the employees.

The industries where women entrepreneurs are playing an active role: manufacturing, pickles, incense sticks, embroidery, handicrafts, apparels, food and beverage services, dry cleaning, flower shops, women health clubs, gyms, hostels, tutorial classes, and so on.

According to Harbison (1956), women entrepreneur engaged in the following five functions:

• Exploring the prospects of initiating a business enterprise.
• Undertaking the risks and economic uncertainties associated with the business.
• Introducing the innovations or imitating them in the business.
• Coordinating, administering, and controlling the business.
• Supervising and providing leadership to the business.

## Features of women entrepreneurs

- *Responsibility*: Women entrepreneurs possess a deep sense of responsibility towards the results of their business.
- *Creativity*: Women entrepreneurs are imaginative, creative, and innovative. They have a favourable approach towards something that is new and are not shy to explore the unexplored.
- *Perseverance*: Women entrepreneurs have a lot of patience to succeed and are determined to achieve the goal even if it means to make further efforts.
- *Optimism*: Women entrepreneurs are optimistic and remain confident in the long run. They try to turn the challenge into an opportunity.
- *Smart work*: Women entrepreneurs are known to be smart and hardworking which makes them quick learners from past mistakes. Smartly done hard work tends to make a venture more successful.
- *Adaptive*: Women entrepreneurs are flexible and quick to adjust to the changing demands of the markets. They easily understand the present tastes of the customers and can mould themselves accordingly.
- *Organisers*: Women entrepreneurs are good at organising and can get along in a team easily. This helps to maintain synchronisation and ensure resources are utilised optimally.

## Factors which motivate the women entrepreneurs

- *Wealthy entrepreneurs*: Women entrepreneurs who come from business backgrounds with substantial financial and other resources are willing to take considerable business risks.
- *Economic agents*: It is considered an adventure to start a new business and also to become economically self-reliant. One may even look to grow the family business to improve the prevalent financial state of the family.
- *Rural-based entrepreneurship*: The entrepreneurship which exploits locally available resources for profit, e.g., dairy products, poultry, pickles, bed sheets, fruit juices.
- *Entrepreneurs who are self-sufficient*: Most of the entrepreneurs concentrated in rural areas and small towns put up a lot of endeavours for the sustenance of their business often due to limited financial resources, e.g., vegetable and fruit vendors. Climate, government schemes, and subsidies are important for such entrepreneurs.

## Ilahi (2012) described various challenges that women entrepreneurs face in India

- To obtain the required financial support.
- Unavailability of raw materials due to the competition.
- Unlike men, women entrepreneurs lack mobility due to family ties.

- Lack of education and poor awareness about the entrepreneurship scope.
- Male-dominated society and tendency to avoid risks.

### 3.3.6  Corporate Entrepreneurship

Corporate entrepreneurship provides a systematic structure so that companies can innovate and increase their revenues. This also aims to reduce bureaucratic hurdles so that a healthy work culture can be sustained.

**Advantages**

- *Growth*: Corporate entrepreneurship makes sure that there are regular updates and enhancements are available to the products and services of the company. This will help to generate higher revenues and future growth.
- *Competitive advantage*: Consistent growth and higher revenues put the organisation ahead of the competitors by achieving a higher quality of the products and services.
- *Recruitment and retention*: The best talent available in the market wants to work in such organisations. The existing employees are encouraged to pursue their interests and are given a good work-life balance. This helps in the retention of employees and helps the organisation to keep attrition rate low.
- *Productivity and personnel morale*: Corporate entrepreneurship improves the work culture and helps the personnel stay motivated. This keeps employees engaged and results in higher productivity.

### 3.3.7  Digital Entrepreneurship

Digital entrepreneurship focuses on changing the dynamics of entrepreneurship through digital technology. European Commission (2015) opined that digital entrepreneurship is engaged in creating new ventures and transforming existing businesses by developing novel digital technologies and/or novel usage of such technologies.

Digital entrepreneurship brings innovative mechanisms to identify opportunities, manage risks, increase market share and productivity, and so on. It also acts as a catalyst for economic growth, employment generation, research and development, and so forth. Today, digital entrepreneurship has made inroads in every aspect of entrepreneurial activities.

### 3.3.8  Health Entrepreneurship

Entrepreneurs working in the health and biomedical domain aim to create value by bringing innovation through digital medical services such as delivering medicines, doorstep health check-ups, online doctor appointments, and so on. These innovations have made these services affordable with a wider reach. With greater access to information and communication technologies (ICTs), people are getting aware of digital platforms providing health and medical services. Some of the prominent start-ups in this domain are 1 mg, Netmeds, Apollo Pharmacy, and so on (Maji, 2020).

## References

Ashoka Fellow Sujay Santra. Retrieved August 19, 2020, from www.ashoka.org/en-in/fellow/sujay-santra/

The Collected Works of Mahatma Gandhi. (2000). India: Publications Division, Ministry of Information and Broadcasting, Government of India.

Danhof, C. H. (1949). Observations on entrepreneurship in agriculture. *Change and the entrepreneur*, Cambridge: Harvard University, 20–24.

European Commission. (2015). *Digital transformation of European industry and enterprises*. A Report of the Strategic Policy Forum on Digital Entrepreneurship.

Harbison, F. (1956). Entrepreneurial organization as a factor in economic development. *The Quarterly Journal of Economics*, 364–379.

Ilahi, S. (2012). Women entrepreneurs in India: Socio economic constraints. *SSRN Electronic Journal*, 2129402.

Kumar, S. A. (2008). *Entrepreneurship development*. New Delhi: New Age International.

Maji, N. (2020, December 12). *E-pharmacy: The growth story of 2020*. Retrieved December 21, 2020, from www.businessworld.in/article/E-pharmacy-The-Growth-Story-of-2020/12-12-2020-352919/

Nobel Peace Laureate: Kailash Satyarthi. Retrieved August 25, 2020, from www.kailashsatyarthi.net/

Shanthi, S. (2020). *The past, present and future of EdTech start-ups*. Retrieved August 13, 2020, from https://inc42.com/features/the-past-present-and-future-of-edtech-startups/

Village Industries. Retrieved July 25, 2020, from www.kvic.gov.in/kvicres/village.php

Women Entrepreneurship. Retrieved July 18, 2020, from www.startupindia.gov.in/content/sih/en/women_entrepreneurs.html

Yunus, M., & Jolis, A. (2003). *Banker to the poor: Micro-lending and the battle against world poverty*. New York: PublicAffairs.

# 4 Entrepreneurial Motivation and Creativity

Entrepreneurs are driven by motivation, grit, and passion. Motivation is an important ingredient in the success of a venture. Some of the important theories of motivation are Maslow's Need Hierarchy Theory, Herzberg Two-Factor Theory, and so on. Creativity and initiative also play a significant role in entrepreneurial development. Two of the most prominent components of creativity are innovation and invention.

## 4.1 Motivation

Motivation refers to the process which encourages people to transform their thoughts and desires to goal-oriented actions. A highly motivated entrepreneur will be able to make better decisions to ensure higher productivity in the venture. A lot of research has been conducted to find the determinants that motivate people to work. We will discuss some of the popular motivation theories here.

## 4.2 Maslow's Need Hierarchy Model

Abraham Maslow (1943) proposed the 'theory of need hierarchy' that is regarded as one of the most notable theories of motivation. The theory is built on the concept of human needs which are classified into hierarchical order. According to the theory, once a specific level of need is satisfied, it ceases to act as a source of motivation rather it triggers the next higher level. The theory recognises five levels of need.

- *Physiological needs* refer to the essential needs which include food, clothing, shelter, and other bare requisites for survival. Once these needs are satisfied, it leads to the emergence of a higher level of needs.
- *Safety and security needs* are the next levels of needs. It refers to be secured and safe from economic uncertainties or any sort of physical

harm. Money is an important factor in the level, and it motivates the person to work more.

*   *Social needs* refer to the requirement of love, belongingness, camaraderie, community-based interaction, and so on. for an individual. This is the reason which makes an individual to work in groups and to form a life outside work.
*   *Esteem needs* refer to self-respect and self-esteem. These needs cover competence, recognition, self-confidence, knowledge, achievement, and so forth. Esteem needs lead to higher productivity and make an individual indispensable to the organisation. In any case, if these needs are not satisfied it may result in low self-esteem, under confidence, inferiority complex, and so on.
*   *Self-actualisation needs* refer to the pinnacle of all the needs of the individual. It is the concluding step under the model which results in self-fulfilment and materialises the aspirations into reality.

Maslow opined that human needs go along with a set progression of supremacy. There have been some criticisms of the theory. However, the theory remains popular because it is easily understandable.

## 4.3   Herzberg's Two-Factor Theory

Psychologist Frederick Herzberg (1964) proposed a motivation theory known as Herzberg's Motivation Hygiene (Two-Factor) Theory. Herzberg made a psychological study in Western Pennsylvania encompassing 200 accountants and engineers. The study revolved around the following question:

When did the employees feel specifically positive and exceptionally negative about their jobs?

The responses that were studied gave quite interesting inferences. Generally, the positive feelings about their job are related to job satisfaction (motivating factors) and negative ones to job dissatisfaction (hygiene factors).

*   *Motivating factors*: Growth, recognition, responsibility, career advancement, etc.
*   *Hygiene factors*: Working conditions, security, company policies, remuneration, etc.

Herzberg opined that the opposite of satisfaction is not dissatisfaction as separating of dissatisfying factors does not guarantee in making the job satisfying. However, this theory also met with some criticisms on the grounds that it neglects situational variables to motivate an individual.

## 4.4   McClelland's Theory of Needs

David McClelland (1961) propounded this popular theory which is centred on the three needs; achievement, power, and affiliation.

- **Need for achievement**

  This need drives people to compete and work for excellence. Individuals with a higher need for achievement are more productive than those with lower needs.

- **Need for power**

  Individuals with a high need for power look for making an impact and influence others in order to keep things under their control.

- **Need for affiliation**

  An individual has an inclination to forge warm and friendly interpersonal relationships with other people.

## 4.5   Creativity and Entrepreneurship

Creativity refers to the imagination and ingenuity of the individual. An entrepreneur can bring innovation to make lives better. Creative thinking revolves around exploring, examining, and expressing the thought process of an individual. Certain factors such as culture, education, age, and so on can have a considerable influence on creativity. A creative entrepreneur will look for making products with better design and utility. According to Barnard and Herbst (2018), creativity is subjected to intuition. It helps to develop the potential to understand an issue in depth and come up with solutions. Creative thinking helps an individual to work across platforms in an efficient manner. Olsen and Bosserman (1984) have opined entrepreneurs should be able to come up with original ideas alongside implementing them too.

We have discussed some of the creativity-driven approaches to generate impactful ideas here.

- *Attribute listing*—An idea is generated taking both positive as well as negative attributes into account.
- *Big dream approach*—It refers to generating an idea when the related hindrances are not taken into consideration.
- *Brainstorming*—Here, an idea is generated with the formation of a group consisting of 6–12 members. The members freely exchange their thoughts and ideas. A senior member moderates the deliberation where any form of criticism is also not allowed.

- *Checklist method*—An idea is generated by listing down all the relevant points involved.
- *Reverse brainstorming*—Post brainstorming process, the group analyses each of the ideas generated. It is an evaluation step where redundant or repetitive ideas are not selected for further discussion.
- *Synectics*—Prince (1968) and Gordon (1961) are credited for developing this method. It is a problem-solving tool that provokes the creative thinking process in a group with members from different domains. According to the method when an individual tries to find a solution to the problem, he/she should not take anything for granted. One should not be confined to the successful past techniques alone. Moreover, past unsuccessful techniques are not to be completely ignored in the pursuit of seeking a solution. It is somewhat more complicated than brainstorming as it involves several steps.

We are surrounded by creativity everywhere. It can be in the form of advertisements, graffiti, posters, and viral videos. Alongside generating new ideas to solve existing problems, creativity also results in the development of innovative products and services. Thus, it plays an important in shaping entrepreneurship development.

## 4.6   Stages in Creativity

Renowned British psychologist, Wallas (1926) proposed a four-stage creative process based on his exhaustive research. These four stages are discussed below:

- **Preparation**

In the first stage, all the relevant information and knowledge are gathered about the issue from reliable sources.

- **Incubation**

In the second stage, all the ideas and information are allowed to immerse in mind. It helps to foster the subconscious evaluation of all the possibilities out there.

- **Illumination**

In the third stage, one can arrive at the cognizance through linkages across ideas and thoughts. In other words, it refers to finding the solution in an unexpected manner.

- **Verification**

In the fourth stage, the individual critically analyses the creative ideas to judge its relevance. The ideas are further refined and polished before putting them to use.

## 4.7 Innovation and Invention

Innovation brings a meaningful enhancement to a product or service. It adds value to a product with better features and making it more user-friendly. Innovation can even help to bring down the costs of manufacturing with the efficient use of production alternatives. Drucker (1986) opined entrepreneurs use innovation as an important tool. It helps them to take advantage of a change and use it as a launchpad for a new opportunity. According to Fillis and Rentschler (2010), increasing opportunities also results in competition. Thus, creative mechanisms should be in place to sustain and keep the business profitable. A new entrant faces substantial challenges to compete against the established entities in the market. Innovation can be the best bet in such cases for an entrepreneur. This can bring competitive advantage and also helps in differentiating the product or service than the competitors. Innovation also raises the market share of business.

**Sources of innovation**

- Uncontrollable events
- Technological disruptions
- Changes in the market structure
- Demographic shifts
- Changing needs of consumers

**Importance of innovation**

- To carve a niche
- To gain competitive advantage
- To get through uncertain market forces

**Positive attitude towards innovation can be developed through**

- Brainstorming
- Understanding the needs of end users
- Analysing the failures
- Learning at the grassroots level

Innovation is a decisive factor in making a business successful both in generation-old ones and start-ups. Invention outweighs innovation by a substantial margin. As per Section 2(1)(j) of The Patent Act, 1970, 'invention' means a new product or process involving an inventive step and capable of industrial application.

An invention can be composed of various innovations such as novel ideas, thoughts, and creativity. Developing a new product or service which can be deemed as invention pays a lot of dividends to an entrepreneur as it helps to create new markets and builds a great reputation for the venture. Great inventions are known to create a huge impact on culture and society. We can see how the internet has changed every aspect of our lives. Today the way we eat, sleep, learn, travel, and so on revolve around smart technology. The life that we are leading today is something unthinkable even a decade ago. The chances of an invention being successful can increase manifolds when there is a unique combination of innovation and acquaintance.

### 4.7.1   *Left Brain Skills and Right Brain Ideas*

There was a time when it was considered that 'left-brained' people are logical and 'right-brained' people are creative. It was said that a person can think from only one side of the brain.

Researchers have stated that there are divergent functions of the two hemispheres of the brain. The right side of the brain is creative and helps in crafts such as painting and music. The left side is inquisitive and analytical with a preference for scientific pursuits. This led to stereotyping people on the basis of their skills and attributes like calling a scientist 'left-brained' and a sculptor as 'right-brained'. However, recent research conducted by Nielsen, Zielinski, Ferguson, Lainhart, and Anderson (2013) proved there is no existence of people with stronger left- or right-sided brain networks. Both sides of the brain are used in everyday life. A student who is solving mathematical problems alongside listening to music is using both hemispheres of the brain. Both creativity and logic can act as complementary to each other in a given situation. An entrepreneur must be able to make a healthy balance between the two aspects of thinking. An over-emphasis of either creativity or logic can be detrimental to business. A successful entrepreneur is known to use and develop both sides of the brain with experience.

### 4.7.2   *Legal Protection of Innovation*

In order to remain competitive in the market, companies put a lot of attention to the innovation of their offerings. Innovation brings significant enhancements and can be instrumental in making the products and services reach close to perfection. However, the innovation which has resulted due to developing a new technique, method, or knowledge also requires protection so that a third party without any contribution may not take undue advantage of it. This is done by Industrial/Intellectual Property Rights (IPRs) which protects patents, logos, brands, trade secrets, and so on through legal mechanisms.

We will have a detailed discussion about these in Chapter 9 which specifically deals with the legal issues and legislation.

## References

Barnard, B., & Herbst, D. (2018). Entrepreneurship, innovation and creativity: The creative process of entrepreneurs and innovators. *Expert Journal of Business and Management, 7*(1), 107–146.

Drucker, P. F. (1986). *Innovation and entrepreneurship: Practice and principles.* Singapore: Harper & Row Publishers.

Fillis, I., & Rentschler, R. (2010). The role of creativity in entrepreneurship. *Journal of Enterprising Culture, 18*(1), 49–81.

Gordon, W. J. (1961). *Synectics: The development of creative capacity.* New York: Harper & Row Publishers.

Herzberg, F. (1964). The motivation-hygiene concept and problems of manpower. *Personnel Administration, 27*, 3–7.

Maslow, A. H. (1943). A theory of human motivation. *Psychological Review, 50*(4), 370–396.

McClelland, D. C. (1961). *The achieving society.* Princeton: Van Nostrand.

Nielsen, J. A., Zielinski, B. A., Ferguson, M. A., Lainhart, J. E., & Anderson, J. S. (2013). An evaluation of the left-brain vs. right-brain hypothesis with resting state functional connectivity magnetic resonance imaging. *PLoS ONE, 8*(8), e71275.

Olsen, P., & Bosserman, D. (1984, May–June). Attributes of the entrepreneurial type. *Business Horizons, 27*(3), 53–56.

The Patent Act, 1970.

Prince, G. M. (1968). The operational mechanism of synectics. *The Journal of Creative Behavior, 2*(1), 1–13.

Wallas, G. (1926). *The art of thought.* New York: Harcourt, Brace & Company.

# 5 Project and Financial Analysis

A systematic analysis of a project plays an important role in the success of a venture. The preparation of a project report is the first step as it takes all the important elements into account. Evaluation of the project is crucial to determine the feasibility of the project. The two most popular methods of project evaluation are Net Present Value (NPV) and Internal Rate of Return (IRR). The efficient planning for the management and utilisation of the financial resources in a business is called financial planning. Designing the budget and overseeing working capital is part of this. In order to make financial planning effective, an entrepreneur should be well versed with various financial statements such as balance sheet, income statement, cash flow statement, and so forth. To get a better picture of the project, specialised techniques in the form of break-even analysis, profitability analysis, and cost-benefit analysis are employed.

## 5.1  Identification and Selection of Projects

Project management is initiated with the identification and selection process. White and Fortune (2002) opined that there are various methods for project management covering from project inception to project completion. This stage is critical as it will impact the viability and performance upon project completion. A project is shaped with the defined objectives which are to be completed within a specific period and allocated budget. A project can be a:

- Amalgamation of human and non-human resources that are put together to accomplish a specific goal.
- Scientific work plan conceived to achieve a defined target within a fixed time.
- Combination of knowledge, skills, and experience which can mitigate the risk associated with a project alongside improving the chances of success.

- Phases, activities, or tasks which are systematically carried out to achieve something.

Generally, a project involves a proposal and capital investment in order to develop specific goods and services. Identification and selection of projects refer to the careful assessment of the project idea and selecting the project with the highest potential to succeed.

- *Project identification* refers to identifying the project idea which starts when a product-related concept is already in place. Hulme (1995) opined that project identification basically involves bringing out various project concepts and selecting the best one after examining them. An entrepreneur can have some possible project ideas but only the most promising one goes ahead.
- *Project selection* follows the process of project identification. It is a detailed study of every aspect of the project idea. After careful deliberation, the best idea is considered.

Investors are always in the hunt for commercially viable projects to make investments. As project identification is a complex exercise, hence certain approaches are applied to determine the outcome. Various factors such as Government policies, available technology, financial situation, business environment, and so on are considered during project identification and selection.

## 5.2   Project Report

A project report is a document that describes the project proposal and the necessary aspects of the planned activities. It includes information relating to the financial, technical, and production features which makes the project viable. It also helps the entrepreneur to seek funds, loans, and so on from various financial institutions and banks. The project report gives a complete picture of the requirements and costs regarding land, infrastructure, manpower, production process, machinery, power, and so forth.

### 5.2.1   *Contents*

The contents of the project report have a lot of significance as it is essential to create a positive impression to the prospective investors. Naidu and Rao (2010) have suggested some of the following information that should be incorporated in a project report:

- **General information**

  A project report must provide information about the details of the industry to which the project belongs to. It talks about the motives of starting the business alongside products or services to be offered. It provides information about the present status, issues, and future prospects of the project.

- **Executive summary**

  A project report presents the overall picture of the project. It tells about the objectives and provides information regarding capital, production, functioning, and other aspects of the business. It also states the risks and the ways to overcome them to ensure the success of the business.

- **Organisation composition**

  The project report should clearly mention the organisation structure for the project. It should indicate the type of ownership of the proposed business, details about the management team, experience of the promoters, obligations of the members, and policies of the business.

- **Project description**

  A project report must present a lucid description of the site location, workplace specifications, manpower requirements, and environmental implications about the project.

- **Production plan**

  Project reports also give details about the technical features of a project such as plant machinery, equipment, technology, production process, and so on. In the case of a service-based business, the details about the services offered must be clearly stated in the report.

- **Marketing plan**

  A project should also mention the demand prospects, strategies, and price of the product or service the business intends to offer. The details about the after-sales support are also to be stated. In other words, there should be a comprehensive marketing plan in place including the costs to execute such a plan.

- **Financial plan**

  The project report must feature a detailed picture of the financial details of the project. It should describe the total capital requirements, working capital required, sources of finance alongside details about owners' and borrowed funds. It must present a projected profit and loss account, balance sheet alongside the estimated rate of return and break-even point.

- **Project implementation**

A project report presents a time frame for the execution of a project. It tells about the time required for the completion of tasks regarding the project. Project implementation takes all these factors into account so that the necessary preparation can be completed in time. It should also keep the social responsibilities and obligations into consideration.

### 5.2.2   *Formulation*

Project formulation involves the structured progress towards the conversion of a project idea into reality. According to Kumar (2008), following aspects should be taken into account during the formulation of a project report.

- *Economic aspect*: The project report should provide adequate details in economic terms regarding the feasibility of the project. The market analysis should also be conducted to ascertain the demand and expected returns about the product/service intended to offer.
- *Financial aspect*: The project report is also supposed to disclose matters related to total investment, sources of finance, and contributions made by the promoters. It should also give a comparative analysis of total capital investment and returns on investment.
- *Technical aspect*: The project report must present a clear picture of the raw material availability, technology to be employed, equipment, machinery, and the production process.
- *Managerial aspect*: The project report should also describe about the policies by which the business is being planned to be managed. It should also mention the relevant experience and educational qualifications of the promoters.

## 5.3   Project Evaluation

According to Smal (1998), project evaluation is generally found in the context of a broader decision-making process. It refers to the structured and scientific appraisal of a project. It helps to ascertain the objectives, effectiveness, and sustainability of the project in long term. It is important for taking decisions and formulating the policies regarding investments, planning, and the related aspects by the stakeholders.

**Objectives of project evaluation:**

- To ensure smooth implementation of the project
- To ensure the highest quality of products and services offered

- To analyse the project performance by ensuring optimal utilisation of resources
- To identify the risks involved in the project and ways to mitigate them

## 5.4   Methods of Project Evaluation

Some of the important project evaluation methods suggested by Remer and Nieto (1995a) are as follows:

- NPV method
- IRR method
- Profitability analysis method
- Cost-benefit analysis method

### 5.4.1   NPV Method

NPV method is applied to determine the present value of the total future cash flows that will be generated by a project. It is widely used to ascertain the profitability of projects.

$$NPV = TPV - \text{Total investment}$$

Where, TPV is Total Present Value

**Criteria of acceptance or rejection of a project:**
- The project is accepted when the value of NPV is greater than zero.
- The project is rejected when the value of NPV is less than zero.
- When the value of NPV is found to be zero then the acceptance or rejection of a project will be decided on the basis of priority or other contingent factors.

**Advantages:**
- It is widely practiced as it helps the promoters to minimise and mitigate the costs associated with a project.
- It takes the time value of money into consideration which makes it a preferred method to evaluate the proposal for capital investment.
- It also takes all the cash inflows of the project into account. It assesses the current value of cash inflows by applying a discount rate that is equal to the capital cost.

**Disadvantages:**

- It is considerably difficult to determine, understand, and implement the capital cost concept.
- It may not provide dependable results in case of dealing with a number of projects with different life cycles.

### 5.4.2   *IRR Method*

IRR method evaluates a project by comparing the IRR to the minimum required rate of return, which is set by the management of the company. Under the method, the value of NPV of the investment is reduced to zero. IRR is calculated when the sum of discounted cash inflows and cash outflows are equal.

$$IRR = \frac{A + (C - O)}{(C - D) \times (B - A)}$$

where, A is lower discounting factor
B is higher discounting factor
C is TPV taking lower discounting factor
D is TPV taking higher discounting factor
O is initial investment

**Criteria of acceptance or rejection of a project:**

- The project is accepted when the value of IRR is greater than the cost of capital.
- The project is rejected when the value of IRR is less than the cost of capital.
- When the value of IRR is found to be equal to the cost of capital, then the acceptance or rejection of a project will be decided on the basis of priority or other contingent factors.

**Advantages:**

- It takes the concept of the time value of money into consideration.
- The calculation of the cost of capital is not mandatory; this makes it better than the NPV method.
- It takes all the cash inflows and outflows through the entire project life cycle.
- It also aims to maximise the wealth of investors.

**Disadvantages:**

- Calculation and application of the value of IRR is somewhat difficult.
- The method assumes that the cash inflows of a particular project can be reinvested in new projects at the discounting rate.
- In case the projects under consideration vary in terms of life cycle, size, and so on, then the results will also be inconsistent under both IRR and NPV methods.

## 5.5   Financial Planning

Financial planning is responsible for framing effective financial policies of an organisation regarding the administration, procurement, and investment of funds. It determines the funding requirements. It also sets suitable policies, programmes, and budget to ensure the adequate financial health of the firm can be maintained.

**Objectives of financial planning:**

- *Determination of capital requirements*—Both short-term and long-term capital requirements are to be considered which depends on current and fixed cost assets, promotional expenses, and so on.
- *Determination of capital structure*—Capital structure comprises both relative and proportion of capital required to operate the business including decisions on debt-equity ratio and so forth.
- Framing of financial policies related to funds, borrowings, lending, and so on.
- Optimal utilisation of financial resources to ensure the resources are utilised to full potential so that the highest returns on investment are generated.

**Importance of financial planning:**

- It creates harmony between the outflow and inflow of funds so that the stability of the business is maintained.
- It ensures an adequate supply of funds, reduces risks, and uncertainties associated with a business which can result in the long-term stability and profitability of the business.
- It helps in the growth and expansion of business for the long-term sustainability of the business.

### 5.5.1   *Cash Budget*

Cash budget refers to the approximation of cash inflows and outflows over a particular period to assess the magnitude of cash surplus or shortage for operating a business.

**Importance:**

- As cash forms the core of managing working capital. The cash budget helps to bring balance between cash availability and cash expenditures of the business operations.
- The cash budget serves as an important tool for managing cash as it discloses the cases of potential cash surplus and shortages as well.

There are mostly three methods used in the preparation of a cash budget depending on the needs and circumstances under which the business operates.

- Receipts and Payments Method
- Adjusted Earnings Method
- Balance Sheet Method

### 5.5.2   *Working Capital*

Working capital refers to the capital needed to carry out the day-to-day operations in a business such as procuring raw material, routine expenses in the form of rent, advertising charges, wages, salaries, and so on. Working capital plays a central role in the efficient operation of a business. It is the excess of current assets over current liabilities.

**Components of working capital:**

- *Current assets* refer to all those assets which are anticipated to be either consumed or sold due to routine business operations within a year, e.g., prepaid expenses, bills receivable, sundry debtors, closing stock, cash in hand and cash in bank.
- *Current liabilities* are those dues that are to be paid to creditors within a year, e.g., sundry creditors, bank overdraft, tax payable.

**Types of working capital:**

- *Gross working capital* refers to the total value of all current assets of the business.
- *Net working capital* is the excess of current assets over current liabilities.

  Net Working Capital = Total Current Assets − Total Current Liabilities

- *Permanent working capital* refers to the minimum amount of capital either in the form of current assets or cash in order to carry out the business activities.
- *Temporary working capital* is the difference between the net and permanent working capital. It is the additional requirement of working capital to meet a particular exigency(s).

**Advantages of working capital:**

- A business enterprise with adequate working capital can make prompt payments to the creditors that help to build and maintain goodwill.
- A business enterprise with sufficient working capital plays an important role in maintaining the solvency as it ensures an uninterrupted flow of production.
- Good credit standing, high solvency, and adequate working capital enable a business to avail easy loans from banks on favourable terms.
- A business firm with adequate working capital help a business to face market risks in the event of depression, lack of demand, and so on.
- A firm with sufficient working capital can also avail cash discounts on the purchases. This helps to ensure continuous production through the regular supply of raw materials.
- A business enterprise with ample working capital can make regular and consistent payment of wages, salaries, wages, and other routine commitments. This enhances the motivation and efficiency of employees and contribute to the profits of the firm.
- Adequate working capital enables a business enterprise to pay regular dividends to its investors. This builds a favourable reputation in the market and helps the enterprise to raise additional funds in the future.

## 5.6   Financial Statements

Financial statements provide comprehensive financial information about the economic activities of an organisation. These are used to ascertain the financial position of an organisation at the end of each accounting period. This

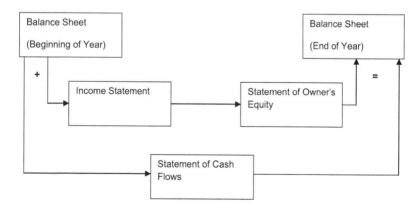

*Figure 5.1* Relationships between financial statements

helps investors and stakeholders to take the necessary financial decisions. Financial statements encompass balance sheets, income statements, cash flow statements, and statements of owner's equity.

### 5.6.1 Balance Sheet

- A balance sheet shows the company's financial position on a particular date.
- It portrays the assets, liabilities, and net worth of the company.
- The balance sheet equation is: Assets − Liabilities = Stockholders' Equity

### 5.6.2 Income Statement

- It shows the operating performance of a company for a given period and acts as a link between the two successive balance sheets of a company.
- Balance sheet and income statement portray the wealth and performance of the company respectively.
- The income statement provides an account of the operating results of a company which is reflected in the equity on the balance sheet in the given accounting period.

### 5.6.3 Cash Flow Statement

- A cash flow statement provides synopsis of the cash or its equivalents entering and leaving a business enterprise. It acts as a supplement to the balance sheet and income statement.
- It tells about the cash management of the business alongside how it generates cash, pays debt obligations, and funds the operating expenses.

The statement of owner's equity reports the alterations in the owner's capital during an accounting period.

The analysis of financial statement involves the following steps:

**Step 1:** Find out the necessary information from the data available in financial statements and other sources.
**Step 2:** Arrange the information in a suitable order.
**Step 3:** Evaluate and infer the information to draw final conclusions.

## 5.7   Break-Even Analysis

Break-even analysis takes the costs of operating the business and selling the price of a product into account to determine the number of sales to achieve break-even. It helps the entrepreneurs to minimise the risks associated with the business. The break-even chart portrays the amount of sales volume at which total costs and total income of the company are identical. At the break-even point, the total costs of the company are equal to its total revenue. A company will incur losses if it operates below the point and will make profits if it operates above the point.

In the graph, OA reflects the income variation at the different levels of output and OB reflects total fixed costs in the business. P is the break-even point where costs and income are equal, that is, a company makes neither profit nor loss.

- *Fixed costs* do not vary with the level of production or output. They tend to remain the same even though the output is zero or high, e.g., factory rent, administration costs, depreciation.
- *Variable costs* vary with the level of production or output, e.g., fuel, raw materials, direct labour.

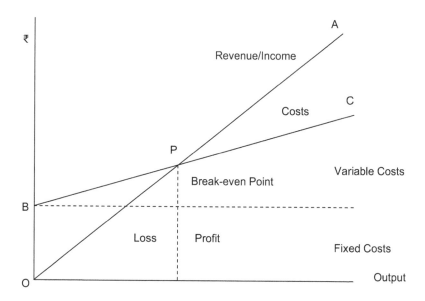

*Figure 5.2* Break-even chart

## 5.8 Profitability Analysis

Profitability analysis is used by entrepreneurs to:

- Predict the profitability of future projects.
- Improve the profitability of present projects.
- Identify most or least profitable customers, products, or services.
- Design an effective product to increase market share and maximise profits.
- Adapt to changing customer demands and preferences.

### *Profitability index method:*

The profitability index (PI) is used to rank investments and it helps to select the best investment that is to be made. It is the ratio of the present value of future cash flows and the initial cash investment.

$$PI = \frac{\text{Present value of future cash inflows}}{\text{Initial investment}}$$

### Criteria of acceptance or rejection of a project:

- The project will be accepted if the value of the PI is greater than one.
- The project will be rejected if the value of PI is less than one.
- When the value of PI is equal to one, then the acceptance or rejection of a project will be decided on the basis of priority or other contingent factors.

## 5.9 Cost-Benefit Analysis

It refers to the approach in which an entrepreneur analyses the expected profits against the costs involved in a project to determine the feasibility of the project. The entrepreneur will go ahead if the estimated returns seem to be greater than the investment made. The cost-benefit analysis involves the following steps:

### *Step 1: Determination of the goals*

First of all, the entrepreneur should have clarity regarding the expectations and goals of the project.

### *Step 2: Understanding the costs and benefits*

Following the setting of goals, the entrepreneur should make a comprehensive evaluation of the costs and benefits associated with the project. Generally, the costs involved are classified into:

- *Direct costs*: direct material, direct labour, manufacturing expenses, inventory, etc.
- *Indirect costs*: rent, electricity, utilities, etc.

Benefits also include the increase in sales and revenue in the event of higher production or introduction of a new product.

### Step 3: Indicate costs and benefits into monetary form

In this step, the entrepreneur will express each of the costs and benefits in terms of monetary values. It is difficult to accurately estimate the future revenues, indirect costs, and so forth especially for a new entrepreneur.

### Step 4: Analyse costs and benefits

Here, the entrepreneur will have to weigh the sum of costs and benefits to take the final decision. If the benefits are found to be higher, the entrepreneur will proceed with the project. If not, then the project warrants further review.

Finally, the entrepreneur will have to calculate the **payback period**. The payback period is the time required to recover the costs of investment or to become break-even. An entrepreneur will always vouch for projects with shorter payback periods.

$$\text{Payback Period} = \frac{\text{Total Cost}}{\text{Total Revenue}}$$

### Limitations of cost-benefit analysis

- The cost-benefit analysis ignores the time value of money, that is, the worth of today's money is higher than the same amount of money one may receive in the future as one can invest and generate income from today's money. The analysis is enough for taking decisions regarding small- and mid-sized projects which take relatively less time to complete. However, for large-sized projects, the analysis alone cannot be appropriate as it may not be able to consider interest rates, depreciation, inflation, and so on.
- In order to perform a cost-benefit analysis, certain assumptions are made as all the necessary data may not be available at a time. This can be difficult for a first-time entrepreneur. Moreover, certain aspects of a project such as customer loyalty, brand value, employee morale, and so forth cannot be estimated accurately in monetary terms. It may result in ineffective analysis and decision-making.

Cost-benefit analysis is often favoured for determining the project worth. However, for complex and critical projects, an entrepreneur should use NPV and the IRR methods.

# References

Hulme, D. (1995). Projects, politics and professionals: Alternative approaches for project identification and project planning. *Agricultural Systems, 47*(2), 211–233.

Kumar, S. A. (2008). *Entrepreneurship development*. New Delhi: New Age International.

Naidu, N. V. R., & Rao, T. K. (2010). *Management and entrepreneurship*. New Delhi: IK International Pvt Ltd.

Remer, D. S., & Nieto, A. P. (1995a). A compendium and comparison of 25 project evaluation techniques. Part 1: Net present value and rate of return methods. *International Journal of Production Economics, 42*(1), 79–96.

Small, K. A. (1998). Project evaluation. In *Transportation policy and economics: A handbook in honor of John R. Meyer* (No. UCTC No. 379). Washington, DC: Brookings Institution Press.

White, D., & Fortune, J. (2002). Current practice in project management: An empirical study. *International Journal of Project Management, 20*(1), 1–11.

# 6 Funding and Organisational Support

The idea about generating funds is pretty important for an entrepreneur because the availability of funds plays the central character in ensuring the success of the venture. The Government of India has also realised the potential of entrepreneurial development and has started various initiatives and programmes to promote it. A lot of specialised organisations have been set up with a focus on entrepreneurship development. Both the State and Central Governments are working together to make these schemes successful. Easy financing of viable projects is also being provided to ensure the creation of employment opportunities and development of the area where the venture is located. Moreover, the Government has also established industrial parks and special economic zones (SEZs) to attract companies to establish their base by providing rewarding incentives.

## 6.1 Sources of Funding for Entrepreneurs

Funding a business plays a crucial role in the success of a venture. It is a challenge faced by most entrepreneurs while financing a start-up. There are basically two types of financial needs—fixed capital requirement and working capital requirement. It is a favourable situation when there are diverse sources of raising funds. However, in the case of proprietorship or partnership ventures, funds are mostly raised through personal sources and also borrowed from banks, friends, relatives, financial institutions, and so on. In the case of large ventures where a substantial amount of equity finance is needed, corporation form of ownership is adopted where all the shareholders contribute to the owners' equity. Bellavitis, Filatotchev, Kamuriwo, and Vanacker (2016) suggested various sources available for entrepreneurs. There are two important sources of funds irrespective of size or operation of the business:

- Internal sources
- External sources

Internal sources of funds are generated from within the business. In the case of start-ups, internal source signifies the capital invested by the owner, partners, and so on. Personal loans are also availed by the entrepreneur. Whereas in the case of enterprises that are already operational, funds are generally raised through the collection of receivables, disposing of surplus inventories, and so forth.

It is a fact that for small-scale enterprises there is a somewhat limited scope for generating funds from the internal sources. External sources of funds like term loans from commercial banks, financial institutions, or borrowing from friends and relatives are generated from outside of the enterprise especially when a huge amount of investment is involved. External sources of funds have considerable risks and costs involved as it may require to mortgaging of the assets as security. Shenoy (2019) suggested some of the following ways by which an entrepreneur can secure funding for his/her start-up.

### 6.1.1   *Bootstrapping*

It refers to self-funding the enterprise and is an effective way to start a business. This is one of the most common practice among first-time entrepreneurs who face difficulty in generating funds for their start-up. Before starting an entrepreneurial venture, most of the budding entrepreneurs wait until a sizeable amount of funds are accumulated by them. However, personal savings may not be always enough to meet all the associated expenses. It is always preferable to use self-funding alongside other sources of funding. Bootstrapping can be pretty advantageous especially when the required amount of initial funding is low. It may not be the right choice for the start-ups which require a huge initial investment. Schinck and Sarkar (2012) opined bootstrapping to be the effective utilisation of resources for the inception of a business which is significant in case of unavailability of credit.

### 6.1.2   *Crowd Funding*

Crowd funding is a new trend of start-up funding which has gained a lot of popularity. According to Kirby and Worner (2014), crowd funding involves the raising of money from individuals or organisations in order to fund a project through an online platform. Under this, the proposed venture seeks loans, funds, or investments from a lot of individuals in a given time. Here, the entrepreneur gives a detailed presentation about the objectives, strategies, product/service offered, and so forth regarding the business for which he/she looking for crowd funding. It helps prospective investors to decide whether to invest money in the business or not. Most importantly, anyone can make an investment if they believe in the business idea as the process is restricted solely to online mode. Some of the famous Indian crowd funding websites are Wishberry, Kickstarter, Fundable, Indiegogo, Milaap, Crowdera, and so on.

### 6.1.3    Angel Investment

Angel investors are those seed investors or individuals with spare capital who invest in promising start-ups for higher returns on their investments. They provide financial backing to start-ups in the early phases in return for ownership equity. They also invest through equity crowd funding and at times also work in networking groups to jointly screen and take decisions about the proposals. Besides capital, they are also known to offer mentorships to the start-ups. Google and Alibaba are two of the biggest companies today which have received extensive financial support during their initial stages. In comparison to traditional investors, angel investors often take greater risks when it comes in making investments. Some of the notable Indian angel investors are Indian Angel Network, Axilor, India Accelerator, and so on.

### 6.1.4    Venture Capital

Venture capital is specifically designed for projects which involve advanced technology and greater risks but also have chances of greater returns. The kind of funding is offered to ventures in exchange for their ownership. Under this, first of all, projects with new products, concepts, or technology are identified which is followed by taking decisions regarding whether to make investments or not. Venture capital may be considered apt for enterprises that have started generating revenues and are not in the early stages. Some of the prominent Indian venture capitalists are Nexus Venture Partners, Kalaari Capital, Accel Partners, Blume Ventures, and so on.

### 6.1.5    Financial Institutions

Financial institutions are one of the important sources of term loans both at state as well as national levels. The aim of establishing financial institutions across the country is to felicitate the availability of funds to business establishments. Both loan capital and owned capital are provided based on the requirements. These institutions are responsible for promoting industrial development in the nation. Alongside providing financial support, these institutions also conduct market surveys and business support to those who are indulged in business.

Some of the prominent financial institutions working at the national level are:

- National Industrial Development Corporation (NIDC)
- Small Industries Development Bank of India (SIDBI)
- Industrial Development Bank of India (IDBI)
- Industrial Finance Corporation of India (IFCI)
- Industrial Credit and Investment Corporation of India (ICICI)

Some state-level financial institutions are:

- State Small Industries Development Corporations (SSIDCs)
- State Finance Corporations (SFCs)

### 6.1.6   Bank Loans

Commercial banks play an important role in providing funds to entrepreneurs with varying purposes and time periods. Banks are seen to be the first place whenever entrepreneurs look to seek funds. Banks offer funding by means of term loans, cash credit, and an overdraft. The loans are granted against adequate securities along with the applicable interest rates.

In most cases, term loans are given for specific purposes which can be for the funding of capital assets, for example, plant machinery. For short-term working capital, cash credit acts as a preferred source. Overdraft schemes which are subjected to applicable terms and conditions can also be useful in certain cases. Some of the prominent commercial banks in India which provides attractive funding options to entrepreneurs are PNB, SBI, IDBI, ICICI, and so on.

### 6.1.7   Trade Credit

Trade credit is a means of short-term financing where one trader offers credit to another to procure goods and services of the former without immediate payment. This is due to the goodwill and mutual understanding between the traders. In accounting terms, the buyers of goods and services are called sundry creditors. The credit amount and the time period can be extended as per the contingencies such as financial position, purchase quantities, payment dues, and so forth. Some of the advantages of trade credit are as follows:

- It results in continuous accumulation and flow of funds.
- It can be easily procured as the customer is acquainted with the seller.
- It involves lesser risks and costs in comparison to most other sources of funding.

### 6.1.8   Issue of Share

The total capital of a business is split into small parts known as a share. The amount of capital that is generated by issuing shares is known as a shared capital. It is divided in two types:

*   **Equity share**

    Funds raised through issuing equity shares are called the owner's fund which is considered as a dependable means for a long-term capital. Equity shareholders also have the ownership of the company with voting rights and occupy management positions of the company.

*   **Preference share**

    Preference shareholders receive fixed dividends, and the payment takes priority over equity holders. The capital which is raised through issuing preference shares is known as preference share capital. In most cases, preference shareholders are not given voting rights.

### 6.1.9   Debenture

Debenture refers to medium to long-term debt instruments utilised by business organisations to raise money. Debentures are issued by both Government and large corporations on a fixed rate of interest. Before the issue of debentures, credit rating agencies are also required to rate them. Debenture holders do not possess voting rights and also not participate in managing the company. Some of the various types of debentures are secured, convertible, redeemable, and so on.

## 6.2   Role of Government in Promoting Entrepreneurship

Indian Government has taken up various schemes and strategies to promote the favourable conditions regarding entrepreneurship across the nation. Entrepreneurship has a great potential to create jobs due to the unique demographic advantages the country possesses. The Government is encouraging innovation and transformation across diverse sectors such as academia, logistics, health, food, and so on. Women entrepreneurship is also playing an instrumental role in economic growth and women empowerment. According to Jahanshahi, Nawaser, Sadeq Khaksar, and Kamalian (2011), Government policies aimed towards developing local Micro, Small and Medium Enterprises (MSMEs) also help in creation of jobs, increase of income, and reduction of poverty. We will discuss some of the programmes undertaken to nurture entrepreneurship (Govt. Schemes, DPIIT).

### 6.2.1 Atal Innovation Mission

Atal Innovation Mission (AIM) is initiated by the Government to encourage creativity and entrepreneurship in the spheres of cutting-edge innovation and start-ups working with newer technologies. Recently under the programme, Atal Tinkering Laboratories (ATLs) and Atal Incubation Centres (AICs) have been established. ATLs are basically the workspaces where young minds are encouraged to take up hands-on training programmes encompassing STEM (Science, Technology, Engineering, and Math)-related concepts. AICs with their countrywide presence provide state-of-the-art incubation facilities to the emerging and innovative start-ups in terms of infrastructure, capital, and operating support so that the businesses can become both scalable and profitable.

### 6.2.2 Biotechnology Industry Research Assistance Council

The Department of Biotechnology has set up Biotechnology Industry Research Assistance Council (BIRAC) to encourage emerging biotechnology-based ventures. The goal is to develop a value for money ecosystem alongside technically superior products. BIRAC aims to bring high-quality research and making academic research to be industry-ready. It has entered into partnerships with various domestic and international partners to help biotech start-ups and SMEs to develop medical, agricultural, and chemical-related technologies.

### 6.2.3 Department of Science and Technology

The Department of Science and Technology (DST) is responsible for the overall development in the domain of science and technology in the country. It strives to develop tech-based solutions towards improving the quality of life with the help of science and technology. ASEAN-India Science, Technology, and Innovation Cooperation aim to improve collaboration on S&T projects between India and ASEAN countries. It also offers fellowships to the scientific researchers from member countries for carrying out joint research in Indian research institutions.

### 6.2.4 Digital India

This has been initiated with the purpose of making various Government services available in the electronic mode. It aims to bring technological modernisation in the way Government functions and thus, ensuring wider access to its offerings. Moreover, under this scheme, the Government also aims to bring high-speed internet connectivity across the nation. It also strives to make Indian digital space accessible, safe, and efficient along with providing the digital services in regional languages to bring technological parity.

### 6.2.5   Jan Dhan-Aadhaar-Mobile

It is a financial scheme initiated by the Government which involves the direct transfer of subsidies to the bank accounts of the beneficiaries by putting an end to the role of intermediaries. It aims to eradicate the forms of corruption and making financial services accessible. Moreover, the underlying purpose is to ensure complete financial inclusion across the country with special emphasis on the poor, backward regions and marginalised section of the population.

### 6.2.6   Make in India

It aims to transform India into a major hub in manufacturing, design, and R&D. The main aim is to eliminate the bureaucratic and other obstacles to attract potential global manufacturing giants to invest in India. It also aims to promote India as a business-friendly destination. This has given a new impetus to the Indian economy and created a positive environment about the business landscape of the country. The initiative has brought transparent and business-friendly policies to improve the ease of doing business in the country. This has helped in bringing higher investments; cultivating skill development, creativity, and building world-class manufacturing infrastructure.

### 6.2.7   National Skill Development Mission

Ministry of Skill Development & Entrepreneurship (MSDE) has initiated the mission to promote skill development across the nation through short-term and long-term training. Many new courses are being added to National Skill Training Institutes and Industrial Training Institutes in this direction. The underlying objective is to create employment opportunities for the trained and skilled manpower alongside encouraging self-employed entrepreneurs. The mission also aspires to realise the vision of skilled India.

### 6.2.8   Pradhan Mantri Kaushal Vikas Yojana

It is the flagship initiative of the MSDE. It is a Skill Certification initiative that aims to train youth in industry-relevant skills to enhance opportunities for livelihood creation and employability. Individuals with prior learning experience or skills are also assessed and certified as a recognition of their prior learning. Training and assessment fees are borne by the Government under this programme.

### 6.2.9 *Science for Equity Empowerment and Development*

It aims to encourage scientists and employees at a grassroots level to indulge in actionable projects in rural belts. There is a special emphasis to carry out research and innovations in specialised S&T establishments with a focus on rural development. This will make technological and other benefits accessible to the backward areas.

### 6.2.10 *Stand-Up India*

Stand-Up India was launched in the year 2015 which aims to seek economic participation of the underprivileged section of the Indian population. It strives to ensure that the benefits of India's economic growth reach women entrepreneurs alongside those belonging to SC & ST and other marginalised communities. The Stand-Up India platform helps to spread awareness regarding financing and credit information to small entrepreneurs.

### 6.2.11 *Start-up India*

The initiative was launched in January 2016 by the Indian Government to encourage entrepreneurship through expert mentoring and institutionalised support. The approach seeks to create a grid between industry and academia to impart the required training and learning programmes to the aspiring entrepreneurs through various incubators. The initiative wants to create an environment where start-ups can prosper without hurdles by facilitating patent filing, tax benefits, regulatory and, funding issues.

### 6.2.12 *Support to Training and Employment Programme for Women*

It was launched by the Ministry of Women and Child Development to train women who do not have access to formal skill training facilities especially to those residing in rural belts. The initiative offers skill-based training in the areas of handlooms, embroidery, agriculture, food processing, hospitality, IT, and so on. Any women above 16 years of age can take advantage of the benefits offered under the initiative.

### 6.2.13   *Trade-Related Entrepreneurship Assistance and Development*

The Trade-Related Entrepreneurship Assistance and Development programme aims to secure the availability of credit to aspiring women entrepreneurs from underprivileged backgrounds through various non-Governmental organisations (NGOs). Along with financial support, they are also provided with training and counselling facilities to enable them to start their proposed ventures. In simple words, this initiative encourages women to take up non-farming activities.

## 6.3   Important Considerations for an Entrepreneur

We will discuss some of the important considerations for an entrepreneur to ensure the success and long-term feasibility of the venture.

### 6.3.1   *Carry on Business (COB) Licence*

Carry on Business licence is regulated under the Industries (Development & Regulation) Act, 1951. It is applicable in case of a non-industrial undertaking that becomes an industrial undertaking. Small-scale industries (SSIs) must apply for the license on crossing the prescribed investment limits unless specific exemptions are given as per the industrial policies.

### 6.3.2   *Environmental Clearance*

It helps to systematically evaluate the effect of an upcoming project on the people and environment of the location. It aims to mitigate the harmful effects associated, if any, to the maximum extent. It is required to obtain Government clearance for the inception of specific projects. As per Environmental Impact Assessment (EIA) Notification 2006, environmental clearance is compulsory for certain projects that can cause environmental pollution such as mining activities, infrastructure development, power generation, and so on. In India, EIA is legally mandated under the Environment (Protection) Act, 1986. EIA categorises the project under 'Category-A' & 'Category-B'. The projects under 'Category-A' are required to get clearance from the Ministry of Environment, Forest and Climate Change. Whereas the projects under 'Category-B' must get clearance from the State Environmental Impact Assessment Authority. 'Category-B' is further categorised into B1 and B2 projects/units. Projects under the B2 category do not require environmental clearance.

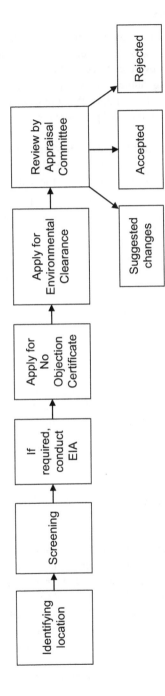

*Figure 6.1* Environmental clearance process

### 6.3.3 Taxation Benefits

Under 'Start-up India' scheme, an entrepreneur should be aware about certain tax provisions. The tax benefits help a new venture to retain money which can be utilised elsewhere. Recent Government policies have been instrumental in providing numerous exemptions and concessions to the entrepreneurs (DPIIT, Govt. of India). We will discuss some of these tax-related benefits available to the entrepreneurs here:

- Start-ups which are certified by Inter-Ministerial Board are given 100 percent tax exemption excluding the Minimum Alternate Tax on income for the period of three years since inception.
- Capital gain taxes are paid by companies with respect to the profits that are earned from company bonds and stocks. However, the start-ups are given 20 percent tax exemption on the capital gain.
- A new venture often faces difficulties in securing funds. Angel investors come to rescue in these circumstances. An agreement about the amount, terms, interest, and so on is reached before making investments. In order to facilitate easier access to capital, Government has made such angel investments tax free.
- As per 'Presumptive Tax Scheme', start-ups with turnover less than ₹2 crore are not required to maintain the books of account that are aimed to provide greater relief to entrepreneurs.

These tax benefits are aimed towards making entrepreneurship an attractive proposition and help entrepreneurs to have more funds at their disposal. Every year the annual budget brings new schemes and policies for the benefit of entrepreneurs.

### 6.3.4 Quality Standards With Special Reference to ISO

The successful ventures often want to increase their revenue and market reach. They also look for expanding to international markets. However, this requires meeting international quality standards and seeking International Organisation of Standardisation (ISO) certifications becomes imperative. ISO provides certification when the organisation and its products meet international quality standards after conducting the rigorous quality assessment tests. ISO standards comprise ISO 9000, ISO 9001, ISO 9002, and ISO 9003 alongside various guidelines about quality management. The ISO 9000 certification signifies the product meets international quality standards and also complies with the relevant regulations. ISO 14000 implies the activities of the enterprise have minimal negative impact on the environment and also meet the prescribed environmental regulations. Availing this certification makes the ventures competitive and improves the credibility in both domestic and international markets. However, the process is quite expensive, especially for start-ups. Therefore, Government has launched the 'ISO 9000/ ISO 14001 Certification Reimbursement Scheme' through the Development Commissioner, Ministry of SSI. This offers a funding scheme for MSMEs to apply for ISO certification under certain terms and conditions (MSME Schemes, Govt. of India).

### 6.3.5 Government Stores Purchase Programme

Government Stores Purchase Programme was launched during 1955–1956 which was aimed towards increasing the share of purchases from the small-scale sector in India. Under the Single Point Registration Scheme, NSIC registers various Micro and Small Enterprises (MSEs) to enable their participation whenever the Government makes purchases. MSEs with less than one year of existence along with Udyog Aadhaar Memorandum are eligible to register. There are various benefits given to MSEs such as free of cost tender information, exemption from earnest money deposit, and so on.

## 6.4 Specialised Organisations for Entrepreneurial Assistance

There are various organisations operating in India both at the national and state levels for the promotion of entrepreneurship. Sathish and Rajamohan (2019) have mentioned some of the important institutions established by the government for the entrepreneurship development in the country.

### National Level

### 6.4.1 NSIC Limited

It was formed in the year 1955 by the Government of India with the aim of providing support to MSMEs. The companies which are registered under NSIC can participate in trade fairs, exhibitions, and also international fairs. This allows these companies to interact with each other. The registered companies can seek funding assistance from banks and also get help in case of procurement of raw materials, technology support, and so on.

### 6.4.2 Small Industries Development Organisation

Small Industries Development Organisation was formed in 1954 with the intention to support the SSIs. It provides various services such as entrepreneurship development training, consultancy, tool making, and so forth.

SIDO helps the Government regarding policy formulation for the growth and development of SSIs. It functions under the Ministry of MSME.

### 6.4.3   SSIs Board

The Board is headed by the Minister in-Charge of SSIs which acts as the highest body responsible to provide advice and recommendations to the Government on the issues encompassing SSIs. The Board includes MPs, State Industry Ministers, Secretaries of Government Departments, industry stalwarts, and others. The board is reconstituted every two years.

### 6.4.4   National Institute of Entrepreneurship and Small Business Development

The organisation was established in the year 1983 and functions under the Ministry of MSME with its headquarters in New Delhi. Its main goal is to promote entrepreneurship and support small industries through consultancy, education, training, and research. It is the highest body responsible for supervising the entrepreneurial development related activities of other agencies as well.

### 6.4.5   National Research Development Corporation

National Research Development Corporation (NRDC) was formed by the Government of India in 1953. Its role is to commercialise and promote the inventions, technologies, patents that are developed by the Universities and R&D institutions. Soundararajan (1983) found the primary condition for NRDC to fund projects is national interest as well as its potential for commercial success. It acts as a reliable source for licensing these technologies to a lot of small and medium scale industries. Moreover, it has also exported the technology, services, machines, and so forth to both developing and developed nations.

### 6.4.6   Khadi and Village Industries Commission

It was established by the Government of India in 1957. It functions under the Ministry of MSME and is the highest body when it comes to the promotion and development of khadi and village industries in the country. It is involved in rural industrialisation and the creation of rural employment to bring self-reliance in rural belts. Katoch (2018) opined that Khadi and Village Industries programme is a great platform for craftsmen operating in rural and backward regions of the country.

### 6.4.7 Small Industrial Development Bank of India

It is headquartered in Lucknow and was formed in 1990 through an Act of Indian Parliament. Its primary role is to promote and finance the small and medium industries. It also provides financial assistance to similar institutions alongside coordinating with their activities. It also actively supports MFIs that are engaged in the development of rural-based enterprises. Rao and Noorinasab (2013) found SIDBI to be playing an instrumental role in identification and addressing the gaps among MSMEs through providing loans, improving capacity building measures, establishing skill development institutes, disseminating necessary information, and so on.

### 6.4.8 Public Sector Banks

Public sector banks play a leading role in shaping entrepreneurship in the country. Some of the leading banks such as SBI, Dena Bank, Union Bank of India, and others have associated with the National Alliance of Young Entrepreneurs. Under these various conferences, programmes, workshops, and so on are conducted for entrepreneurs. Banks are also involved in identifying and supporting potential entrepreneurs with commercially viable projects.

### 6.4.9 National Bank for Agriculture and Rural Development

The financial institution was established by the Indian Government in 1982 with its headquarters in Mumbai. Its main aim is to manage and regulate the credit facilities offered to encourage agriculture, cottage, handicrafts, and so on to ensure the development of rural areas. It is also involved in the formulation of policies towards agriculture and supplement the economic pursuits in the rural belts as well. Goyal (2015) stressed the importance of National Bank for Agriculture and Rural Development regarding policymaking and improving the conditions of rural financial institutions through better utilisation of the available resources.

### State Level

### 6.4.10 State Financial Corporations

SFCs are primarily responsible to ensure the growth of SSIs in the states of their existence. Alongside extending financial support, they encourage higher investments in the sector to create more employment opportunities. Moreover, SFCs also provide assistance to enterprises involved in innovative practices such as poultry farming, tissue culture, engineering, commercial services, and so forth. Sinha (2016) opined that SFCs have immensely contributed to the development of both small-scale industrial sectors as well as overall development of the nation. At present, there are 18 SFCs in the country.

### 6.4.11   State Industries Development Corporation

State Industries Development Corporations (SIDCs) are established to encourage the pace of industrialisation in the states of their existence. These are under the control of State Governments and manage its numerous incentive schemes. SIDCs develop the required infrastructure to develop the industrial areas of the state. They raise funds through reserves, share capital, and other means. At times they also make borrowings from IDBI, State Government and also raise funds through issuing bonds, debentures, and so on. In India, there are 22 SIDCs have been established till date.

### 6.4.12   State Small Industries Development Corporation

SSIDCs have been established to support the small-scale enterprises in the rural and underdeveloped areas in the rural belts in the states of their existence. Some of the important responsibilities of SSIDC are follows:

- Providing financial assistance and marketing support to the products of small-scale enterprises on behalf of the State Government.
- Construction and maintenance of the necessary industrial infrastructure.
- Supplying the required machinery and related services on the basis of the hire-purchase system.

### 6.4.13   West Bengal Industrial Development Corporation Limited

It was established by the Government of West Bengal in 1967 to promote West Bengal as an attractive industrial destination. In order to facilitate the proposals regarding industrial investments, it has formed a single-window agency named '*Silpa Sathi*' or State Investment Facilitation Centre. It functions under the Department of Industry, Commerce & Enterprises to support the industrial development of the state through facilitating the industrial investments and developing the required ecosystem. Every year it organises Bengal Global Business Summit. It is the nodal agency of the state involved in the policymaking and various schemes regarding the growth and development of the industrial sector (WBIDC, Govt. of West Bengal).

### 6.4.14 *West Bengal Industrial Infrastructure Development Corporation*

It is responsible for developing the necessary industrial infrastructure regarding roads, water supply, network connectivity, street lighting, and so on in West Bengal. It has established around 18 Industrial Growth Centres till date encompassing both developed and backward regions of the state. It works under the Department of Industry, Commerce & Enterprises to ensure stable and balanced industrial development in the state.

### 6.4.15 *West Bengal Electronics Industry Development Corporation Limited*

It was established in 1974 to develop the electronics industry of the state. It has played an instrumental role in developing the IT-related infrastructure in West Bengal. In order to promote West Bengal as a premier knowledge hub, it has taken decisive steps to promote the participation of the private sector as well.

## 6.5 Industrial Parks and SEZs

The Government of India has established industrial parks to promote high standards of manufacturing and service delivery at competitive rates in the country. It aims to encourage the private sector to invest in these so that it can give a boost to the Indian economy. This will also help in the creation of a large number of employment opportunities. According to Sampat (2008), development of infrastructure, real estate, and providing incentives to the private developers promote the growth of SEZs. The Government gives lots of tax incentives to the industrial units operating under SEZs. This significantly helps to reduce the costs of the products and services. Many of the obsolete rules and regulations have been removed to promote India as a business-friendly destination. Under the Make in India scheme, 100 percent foreign direct investment is allowed in certain sectors such as single-brand retail trading, e-commerce, railway infrastructure, and so on. SEZ investments are eligible for a 100 percent tax exemption for the first five years and a 50 percent tax exemption for the next five years.

## References

Bellavitis, C., Filatotchev, I., Kamuriwo, D. S., & Vanacker, T. (2016). Entrepreneurial finance: New frontiers of research and practice. *Venture Capital*, *19*(1–2), 1–16.

Department for Promotion of Industry and Internal Trade (DPIIT). *Start-up recognition & tax exemption*. Retrieved August 16, 2020, from www.startupindia.gov.in/content/sih/en/startupgov/startup-recognition-page.html

The Environment (Protection) Act, 1986.

Government Schemes. Retrieved August 26, 2020, from www.startupindia.gov.in/content/sih/en/government-schemes.html

Goyal, P. K. (2015). The role of NABARD in agriculture and rural development: An overview. *International Research Journal of Commerce Arts and Science*, *6*(10).

The Industries (Development & Regulation) Act, 1951.

Jahanshahi, A. A., Nawaser, K., Sadeq Khaksar, S. M., & Kamalian, A. R. (2011). The relationship between government policy and the growth of entrepreneurship in the micro, small & medium enterprises of India. *Journal of Technology Management & Innovation*, *6*(1), 66–76.

Katoch, G. (2018). A Khadi and Village Industries Commission: Role, challenges and opportunity ahead. *Pacific Business Review International*, *11*(2), 79–87.

Kirby, E., & Worner, S. (2014). *Crowd-funding: An infant industry growing fast*. Madrid: IOSCO Research Department.

Ministry of Environment and Forests (MoEF). *Environmental impact assessment notification 2006*. Retrieved August 18, 2020, from www.indiaenvironmentportal.org.in/content/ 265655/environmental-impact-assessment-notification-2006/

MSME Schemes: How you can benefit from ISO 9000/ISO 14001 Certification Reimbursement Scheme. Retrieved August 21, 2020, from https://economictimes.indiatimes.com/small-biz/money/msme-schemes-how-you-can-benefit-from-iso-9000/iso-14001-certificationreimburs-ementscheme/articleshow/70532407.cms

National Institute of Entrepreneurship and Small Business Development (NIESBUD): Ministry of Skill Development and Entrepreneurship: Government of India. Retrieved July 16, 2020, from www.msde.gov.in/organizations/niesbud

Rao, K. S., & Noorinasab, A. R. (2013). The role of SIDBI in developing the MSMEs in India. *IOSR Journal of Economics and Finance*, *1*(6).

Sampat, P. (2008). Special economic zones in India. *Economic and Political Weekly*, 25–29.

Sathish, A., & Rajamohan, S. (2019). Role of industrial promotional agencies in India for the entrepreneurship development. *ZENITH International Journal of Multidisciplinary Research*, *9*(6), 455–463.

Schinck, A., & Sarkar, S. (2012). Financial bootstrapping: A critical entrepreneurship skill. *Centro de Estudos e Formação Avançada em Gestão e Economia da Universidade de Aveiro*, *20*, 1–24.

SEZs. Retrieved December 29, 2020, from www.india.gov.in/topics/commerce/sezs

Shenoy, S. (2019, May 25). *The ultimate guide for entrepreneurs to get startup funding in India*. Retrieved July 26, 2020, from https://yourstory.com/2019/05/startup-funding-entrerpreneur-guide-crowdfunding-equity-debt.

Single Point Registration Scheme. Retrieved July 28, 2020, from www.nsic.co.in/Schemes/Single-Point-Registration

Sinha, J. (2016). Role of state financial corporations: An analysis of various committee reports. *Splint International Journal of Professionals*, *3*(5), 85.

Soundararajan, P. (1983). Research development and transfer of technology approach by the National Research Development Corporation of India. *Technovation*, *2*(1), 55–60.

West Bengal Electronics Industry Development Corporation Limited. Retrieved August 28, 2020, from www.webel.in/about-webel

West Bengal Industrial Development Corporation. Retrieved August 28, 2020, from www.wbidc.com/about-us/overview

West Bengal Industrial Infrastructure Development Corporation. Retrieved August 28, 2020, from www.wbiidc.org/profile.php

# 7    Business Plan Development

A business plan is not a fixed document but rather a dynamic one. It's a shared vision between the entrepreneur and the team members about where the business is at present, where it plans to go, and how it plans to reach there in the future. A good business plan will bring in talents, partners, investors, and government support and will also help in smooth operations of the business. It also helps in identifying the financial, human resources, and marketing needs of the business. There are various methods available to frame a business plan.

## 7.1  Introduction

Business plan is an important step towards building a successful venture. A business plan refers to the sequence of steps to attain a specific objective. A business plan can be initiated with a simple question like how many units of products the entrepreneur desire to sell in a year. The numbers decided should be achievable that should be determined on the basis of market research. In order to achieve these sales targets, the competent manpower should be in place. The team should have the right combination of marketing, finance, and human resource personnel. According to Lall and Sahai (2008), a meticulously designed business plan can transform an elementary idea into a successful business venture.

## 7.2  Business Plan

It provides an outline to achieve business goals. This is not merely a one-time plan rather it is an active component which undergoes continuous modifications with respect to the changes in business and market forces. It is not confined to marketing, finance, operations, sales, or any specific domain. A business plan is multidisciplinary and multifaceted in nature which takes different standpoints into consideration. It also serves as a proposal for investors, credit agencies, and stakeholders to get involved in the business. The business plan reflects both short-term and long-term goals. This is a complete roadmap for business growth and development. It connects the entrepreneur with the investors, venture capitalists, and banking institutions by providing the required foundation for investment.

### *Need of a business plan*

Business plan evaluates the readiness and feasibility of the business venture for the market. In the long run, it will keep track of the required activities to ensure survival and be a market leader in the market. It is also advisable to write a business plan when an entrepreneur is:

* Searching for funding, loans, or investments for new or existing business.
* Looking for a new partner.
* Attracting, hiring, and retaining the top talent.

### Purpose of business plan

* It highlights the aspects of the business that require special consideration.
* It helps to make a SWOT analysis of the business.
* It helps in optimal use of financial resources.

Khanka (2006) suggested different names of business plans based on the target audience. A bank may term it to be a 'loan proposal', a venture capital group may call it a 'venture plan' and for a common man it is a 'project report'.

## 7.3  Various Business Models

Before making a business plan, we will discuss two of the popular business models. Business model is the blueprint of how an entrepreneur desire to build a product and the business plan implies the procedure to make the product. The study of these business models helps an entrepreneur to recognise various factors important to operate the business.

### *7.3.1  The Business Model Canvas*

This was suggested by Alexander Osterwalder and Yves Pigneur. It has nine segments. Each segment forms the spine of the business, which delivers the essential items to be covered and considered in the operation of the business successfully. The following list with questions will assist an entrepreneur to develop a business model.

1.  **Key partners**

    a.   Who are going to be the key partners of the entrepreneur?
    b.   What is the rationale behind the partnership?

2.  **Key activities**

    a.   What key activities are required in the business?
    b.   What activities are to be done regarding distribution channels, customer relationships, and revenue streams?

3.  **Value proposition**

    a.   What is the core value that is offered to the customer?
    b.   Which of the customer requirements are being gratified?

4.  **Customer relationship**

    a.   What relationship that the target customer desires to establish?
    b.   How can this be integrated into the business in terms of cost?

5.  **Customer segment**

    a.   What values are being created for the customers?
    b.   Who are the important customers of business?

6.  **Key resources**

    a.   What resources are needed in business?
    b.   What resources are important in distribution channels, customer relationships, and revenue streams?

7.  **Distribution channel**

    a.   Which channels will be used to reach customers?
    b.   Which channels are the best for the business? How much do they cost? How can they be integrated into the path of entrepreneurs and customers?

8.  **Cost structure**

    a.   What are the main high-priced areas in the business?
    b.   Which of the crucial resources/activities are mainly expensive?

9.  **Revenue streams**

    a.   What is the value that customers are willing to pay?
    b.   What is their preferred mode of payment?
    c.   How much does each revenue stream add to entire revenue?

### 7.3.2 The Lean Canvas

Ash Maurya adapted this business plan from the one suggested by Alexander Osterwalder. The plan aims to eliminate the losses in terms of time, inventory, resources, and so on. The lean canvas is a concise and comprehensive one-page format streamlined for lean start-ups. It implements the same nine blocks concept with enhancements to cater to the needs of lean start-ups. The model is shown below:

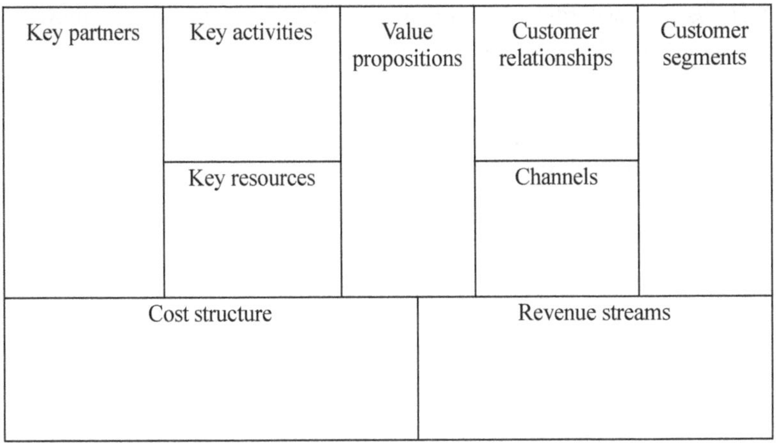

| Key partners | Key activities | Value propositions | Customer relationships | Customer segments |
|---|---|---|---|---|
| | Key resources | | Channels | |
| Cost structure | | | Revenue streams | |

*Figure 7.1* Business model canvas

Source: Adapted from Osterwalder and Pigneur (2010)

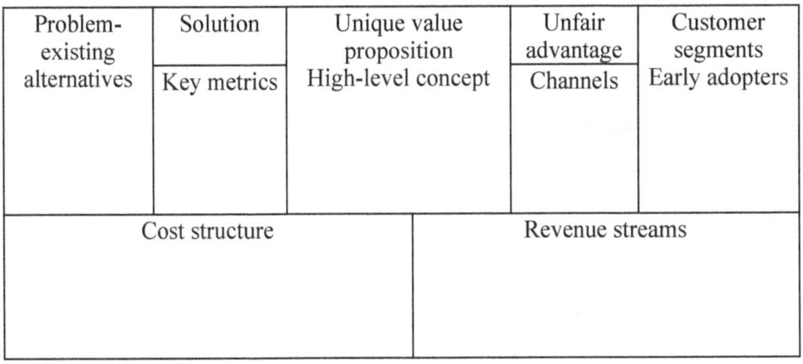

| Problem-existing alternatives | Solution | Unique value proposition | Unfair advantage | Customer segments |
|---|---|---|---|---|
| | Key metrics | High-level concept | Channels | Early adopters |
| Cost structure | | | Revenue streams | |

*Figure 7.2* Lean canvas

Source: Adapted from Maurya (2010)

## 7.4   Structure of a Basic Business Plan

A systematic business plan attracts investors and other talents to the venture. It acts as a proposal for the person reading the plan. Now with the available resources, entrepreneur tries to align plans involving marketing, sales, hiring, operations, and so on with the financial plan. A business plan acts as foundation for determining the mission and vision. It is essential to evaluate the present position of business and make effective plans to reach the desired position. In case of any trouble, the entrepreneur must change the business plan accordingly. Lall and Sahai (2008) suggested the following steps to prepare the structure of a business plan:

- Generation of idea
- Scanning of environment
- Feasibility analysis
- Preparation of project report
- Evaluation, control, and review

## 7.5   Creating a Business Plan

Janakiram and Rizwana (2011) suggested the following elements which should be included in a business plan:

- Executive summary
- Business description
- Marketing
- Operations
- Management
- Financial
- Critical risks
- Harvest strategy
- Milestone schedule
- Appendix

### 7.5.1   *Executive Summary*

The executive summary indicates the overall plan. An executive summary grabs the readers' attention and encourages them to look forward to the entire plan. The summary should be comprehensive with all the pertinent data.

### *How to write an executive summary?*

This is all about the unique value proposition of the business. The objective is to grab the reader's attention through relevant facts and information. The executive summary should be written in such a manner so that it will benefit the employees, partners, and customers. Here are a few points that we cover in an executive summary.

- *Description of business*: Information regarding the product/service the business wishes to offer.
- *The market*: The desired positioning of the product/service and the segments to be covered.
- *Growth potential*: The business potential in the coming years along with those who are associated with the business.
- *Sales and profits forecast*: A summary of the sales and profit forecast figures and the production volume being planned.
- *Financial requirements and its utilisation*: The financial resources and money estimates which would be required to run the business. The plans and strategies in place to spend the money.
- *Repayment of loans and dues*: The expected loan repayment period and other dues.
- *Assistance required*: The assistance and other external help that would be required to launch the business.
- *People*: The plans to get competent people on-board with the desired skill sets.
- *Marketing and sales*: The channels that will help the business to raise market awareness and also improve its reach.

### 7.5.2 General Company Description

This is a description of the business and the business team. The company description contains three elements:

- Mission statement
- History
- Objectives

A mission statement provides the business purpose. It states the objective that the business wants to fulfil. This statement plays a pivotal role in influencing and making connections with people. The mission statement should be easy to understand and outline the purpose of serving the community. It is desirable if the business describes the history or idea behind its creation through the following points:

- Founding date
- Major milestones
- Location or locations
- Number of employees

- Administrative leadership roles
- Leading products or services

Formulating the business objectives gives a defined path and keeps the business on the right track. It also helps to plan out various steps to realise the objectives which should be SMART, that is, specific, measurable, achievable, realistic, and time-bound.

### Example of a company description

Company X is a Kolkata-based agri-business start-up founded in 2016 by Mr. A and Mr. B. It supplies fruits, vegetables, and flowers which are produced through natural and organic methods. The quality of the products earned the business a loyal customer base in the community. The founders have over ten years of combined experience in growing, cultivating, and processing organic food. The employees working here are also given adequate training to ensure customers are provided with quality fruits, flowers, and vegetables.

### 7.5.3   The Opportunity or Competitive Analyses

This is a crucial part where the competitive advantages of the business are written down with respect to the competitors. Competitive research begins by going through the profiles of competitors operating in the market where the concerned business is currently serving or is planning to serve. One must identify them in a chart and build the opportunity that they have been left out. The idea is to carve a path in the minds of the customer so that they become inclined towards the business venture. The prospective entrepreneur must be able to answer these questions after the most significant competitors are identified:

- Where do the competitors bring their products from?
- What kind of products the competitors offer?
- What is the service gap?
- What are the present opportunities in the market?
- How do the competitor stake advantage of the distribution channels?
- What are their sales and pricing strategies?
- How do they rank on third-party rating platforms?

### Example of competitive analysis

Within Kolkata, there are two farms operating within the selected market segments are community-based and focus solely on a few households.

*Table 7.1* Company X and Company Y

| Company X | Company Y |
| --- | --- |
| The average cost per project: ₹2,20,0000 | The average cost per project: ₹3,00,0000 |
| Customer base: 20,000 | Customer base: 35,000 |
| Google My Business Rating: 3.5 stars from 163 reviews | Google My Business Rating: 3.9 stars from 57 reviews |
| Environmental certifications: None | Environmental certifications: None |
| Primary marketing channels: Google Ads | Primary marketing channels: Leaflets and newspaper |
| Service area: 30 km | Service area: 35 km |

### 7.5.4 Market Research and Industry Analysis

Market research is carried out to understand the market, availability of resources, customer preferences, and so on. Industry analysis is done to understand the threats and opportunities so that the right strategy is adopted to address emerging challenges. It is also key to stabilise the business and improve the market share. To identify various market segments, the demographic information of the marketlike the following can be listed:

- Location
- Income
- Age
- Gender
- Education
- Profession
- Hobbies

### Example of market research and potential

The most suitable customers of Company X are those who reside in apartments or homes without any area to build a garden. Nowadays, people are becoming increasingly food conscious and don't shy away from spending money on healthy organic food. The company serves households with medium to high disposable income. Most of the customers are in the age group of 25–55 years who are either working professionals or retired. Market research suggests that Company X will have good prospects in future. The market has witnessed sizeable growth in the past five years regarding the consumption of organic food.

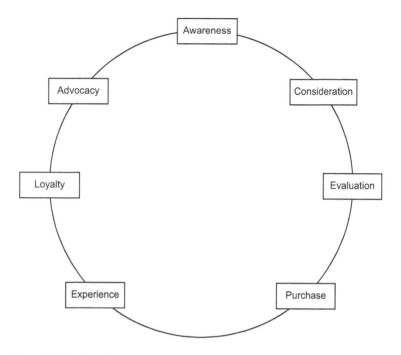

*Figure 7.3* Customer journey map

### 7.5.5   *Strategy*

A strategy helps to bring clarity and refine the leadership vision. It articulates the future goals by acting as a means through which a company intend to achieve them. A strategy helps to ensure optimal utilisation of resources in business. The business environment is very unpredictable and therefore requires analytical reasoning and strategic positioning. Strategic planning helps in the efficient planning of a product, market forces, and manpower in the business. Strategic management comes handy at various levels of the business. Three things we should keep in mind while planning a strategy:

- *Be available*: Always listen and be available to customers which will create a sense of togetherness.
- *Keeping the promise*: The business shouldn't make false promises and should have strong ethos.
- *Sustenance of growth*: There should be plans to keep the business growing along with the plans for sustaining it. A win-win situation should be created for all the stakeholders involved.

It should also describe the benefits, production process, and lifecycle of the product/service and in what ways the business offerings are better than the competitors. The production process should be concerned about:

- Sourcing of raw materials or components.
- Assembling through manufacturing.
- Maintaining quality control and quality assurance.
- Supply-chain logistics
- Managing daily operations: book-keeping and inventory.

**Within the product lifecycle portion, it is important to map elements like:**

- Time between purchases
- Upsells, cross-sells, and down-sells
- Future plans for research and development

### *SWOT analysis*

SWOT analysis is the process of evaluating the internal and external environment of a business by identifying the strengths, weaknesses, opportunities, and threats from other businesses. Chole, Kapse, and Deshmukh (2012) termed SWOT analysis as a scientific approach for assessing the potential for the sustenance and success of a business venture.

*Table 7.2* SWOT analysis

| Strengths | Opportunities |
|---|---|
| The core competencies that give the product or service certain advantages. | Under the right conditions, opportunities can lead to greater growth and profitability. |
| Example: | Example: |
| • High quality<br>• Competitive pricing | • New markets<br>• Export potential<br>• Joint venture proposal |
| **WEAKNESSES** | **THREATS** |
| The areas of the business require improvements. | The possible factors that could adversely affect the business in the future. |
| Example: | Example: |
| • Lack of funds<br>• Lack of management skills<br>• Unskilled workforce | • Imported products<br>• New entrants<br>• Political and economic changes |

### 7.5.6 The Team

A team is a group of people working together towards a goal. It also constitutes the human resources of the business. It is an essential part of the business that comprises various kinds of people with varying skill sets, expertise, and experience. There is a basic concept when choosing a team, that is, they must have an interest in working together towards a common goal. In business, the human resources are categorised into three ways:

- *Top-Level Management (sets goals)*: Founder, CEO, and MD
- *Middle-Level Management (prepares strategy for fulfilling the goals)*: Managers, Assistant Managers, Developer, and Head Designer
- *Lower-Level Management (executes the task to fulfil the goal)*: Staffs and Workers

These people are responsible for various activities and work according to the delegation of authority. Everyone is responsible for their part of the job. It is important to understand and identify:

- How many people with the specific skill set the business require hiring?
- What are the roles of each team?
- Whether the business requires an additional partner?

### 7.5.7 Marketing Plan

Marketing involves the promotion and sale of products/services in the market. It encompasses the following activities:

- Promotion
- Distribution
- Advertising
- Customers relations

All these activities are planned based on the business objective. Following things should be kept in mind during the preparation of marketing plan.

- The product or service
- The customer
- The place
- The method

### 7.5.8   *Operational Plan*

The operational plan deals with the day-to-day activities that are required to be carried out to run a business efficiently. It ensures efficient manpower, marketing, and resource planning. Here, plans about operating the business such as raw material handling, product packaging, and final product delivery are recorded. Some of the important points to be kept in mind while preparing the business plan are as follows:

* Whether business premises are to be taken in rent/lease or purchased?
* Are the current premises easily accessible to work?
* Can it support the expansion of workload?
* What machinery is available and the ones required to be purchased in the future?
* Who are the current suppliers/agents of the business?

### 7.5.9   *Financial Plan*

Financial plan helps the business to acquire the required money. It also helps in devising plans for its expenditure and investment. Capital management is a crucial component of running a business as there are various kinds of costs involved in a business:

* *Start-up cost or setup cost*: The cost that will be incurred in setting up a business.
* *Fixed cost*: The cost that will be used in the business irrespective of the sales volume or any other activity.
* *Variable cost*: The cost that will vary with the changes in production output.
* *Direct cost*: Cost that is directly involved in the production process or cost that is involved in the core business process, For example, labour, land, material, and shipping.
* *Indirect cost*: Cost that is required to support the business-like rent, electricity, service charges, and so on. These costs add up to business and makeup the whole business budget.
* *Working capital fund*: The fund required to run daily business activities.

### 7.5.10   *An Appendix*

An appendix contains additional documents and resources that are not included in the above elements. It may consist of documents such as trade agreements, government licenses, patents, IPRs, marketing brochures, details of the team, and so forth.

A business plan should be written in a presentable manner. It should be printed using good quality papers with a well-designed layout.

# References

Chole, R. R., Kapse, P. S., & Deshmukh, P. R. (2012). *Entrepreneurship development and communication skills*. Jodhpur: Scientific Publishers.

Janakiram, D. B., & Rizwana, M. (2011). *Entrepreneurship development: Text and cases*. New Delhi: Excel Books.

Khanka, S. S. (2006). *Entrepreneurial development*. New Delhi: S. Chand Publishing.

Lall, M., & Sahai, S. (2008). *Entrepreneurship*. New Delhi: Excel Books.

Maurya, A. (2010, August 11). *How I document my business model hypotheses*. Retrieved September 16, 2020, from https://web.archive.org/web/201008150 74344/www.ash maurya.com/2010/08/businessmodelcanvas/

Osterwalder, A., & Pigneur, Y. (2010). *Business model generation: A handbook for visionaries, game changers, and challengers*. New Jersey: John Wiley & Sons.

# 8  Introduction to Research

Research comprises activities towards investigation for the reason of gaining knowledge from new facts. There should be a systematic search by applying scientific techniques to solve a particular problem, finding new facts, or improvement of a certain situation. The scope of entrepreneurship development research is huge. Entrepreneurship development research has the potential to provide new insights into the unorganised entrepreneurship development process and structure in India. The research can provide new insights to improve the prevailing theories through scientific methods. It can be instrumental to establish new theories and techniques for exploring the new areas in entrepreneurship development. In this chapter, we have discussed some of the basic concepts of research methodology which can be helpful to entrepreneurs in case they go for further research in the domain.

## 8.1  Classification of Data

First, we need to understand the concept and classification of data. Data are nothing but the collection of facts, such as observations, numbers, measurements, words, or descriptions of things. Hox and Boeije (2005) suggested the following types of data that we mostly use in research.

- *Primary data* refer to the original data that are collected for the purpose of a particular research objective.
- *Qualitative data* involve the cognizance of specified attributes in the research setting such as interview transcripts, field notes, and so on.
- *Quantitative data* refer to the data that can be expressed in numerical terms such as objects, variables, and so forth.
- *Secondary data* may be collected for a different purpose but can be reused for another research context.

## 8.2   Classification of Variables

A variable refers to a characteristic of an object of study. Pokhariyal (2019) described the variables in following ways:

- *Independent variable* measures the factor that is presumed to influence the outcome in a study. It helps to describe the other variables which are used in the study.
- *Dependent variable* measures the outcome in a study and is described by other variables.
- *Moderating variables* influences the robustness of the relationship between independent and dependent variables.
- *Mediating variables* elucidates the relationship between independent and dependent variables.

## 8.3   Sampling Techniques

According to Acharya, Prakash, Saxena, and Nigam (2013), a 'sample' is a subset of the population that is selected to represent the larger population. We take a sample as it is not possible to study the entire population. Some important terms associated with sampling are as follows:

- *Population element or sampling unit* indicates to a singular representative of the population.
- *Sampling frame* includes properly identified population elements that are accessible to the researcher at any stage of the sampling process.
- *Sampling error* occurs when the sampling elements do not accurately represent the attributes of the population.
- *Non-sampling error* happens due to the incorrect response from the respondents, data analysis error, sampling frame error, and so on.

### 8.3.1   Classification of Sampling Techniques

Sharma (2017) suggested some of the following sampling techniques:

- *Probability sampling* is an unbiased method where the sampling units are taken randomly with each population element having the same possibility of being selected as a sample. It is classified by four different methods:
  - **Simple random sampling**

  Here, each sample element is randomly selected from the population. It shows each population element has equal chances of selection.

- ○ **Systematic sampling**

  In this method, except the random selection of the first element, all other elements are selected systematically. Here, the sample elements are chosen at fixed intervals of population and all the elements are arranged in a sequence. This ensures each element gets equal probability during the selection.

- **Stratified sampling**

  In this method, the population is divided into small subgroups (strata) in such a manner that the elements within the same group are homogeneous in nature. The elements are selected from these strata randomly. However, the researcher should have prior knowledge about the population to be able to form subgroups.

- **Cluster sampling**

  This method is generally used in case of research based on a particular geographic location. Here, also the population is divided into subgroups (clusters). These clusters are randomly selected as sampling units instead of the elements in subgroups.

- *Non-probability sampling* contains certain biases as the selection of sample elements depends on the discretion of the researcher. It is also classified by four different methods:

  - ○ **Convenience Sampling**

    In this technique, interviewers gather the sample element according to their convenience and accessibility. It consumes least costs and resources. Examples include surveys conducted in malls, departmental stores, and so on.

- **Purposive sampling**

  Here, sample elements are selected according to the judgement of the researcher. The researcher feels that the chosen sample elements are appropriate for the research and accurately represent the population.

- **Quota sampling**

  It is a popular method for market research. Here, the selected sample is based on the pre-decided features of the population. The survey population is divided into mutually exclusive subgroups and the researcher selects the sample from each of these subgroups.

- **Snowball sampling**

   This method is used in case of difficulty in identification of sampling frames. Here, existing subjects recommend other subjects acquainted to them which increases the sample size like a rolling snowball.

## 8.4   Concept of Hypothesis

The hypothesis is a statement of assumption which is to be proved statistically. In research, hypothesis testing is required where population parameter(s) is unavailable to decide if the sample data support the research objectives. It helps to create probability statements regarding population parameter(s). An example of the hypothesis:

   'Entrepreneurial growth positively influences the employment opportunities'.

In this case, hypotheses should be verified and tested to fulfil the research objectives related to the problem statement. In other words, it is a proposition to confirm the validity of the problem statement.

### 8.4.1   *Basic Attributes of Hypothesis*

Anupama (2018) described the following characteristics of a hypothesis:

- It should be stated in an understandable and simple language.
- It should be consistent to the established facts from the literature review.
- It should be clear and specific.
- It should be tested within a specific time frame.
- It should indicate some association between variables.

### 8.4.2   *Null and Alternative Hypothesis*

The null hypothesis refers to the assumption of two or more sample data from different populations to be equal. However, if we propose that sample data are not equal to each other ($\neq$ or $<$ or $>$) then it is called the alternative hypothesis. The null hypothesis is denoted by $H_0$ and the alternative hypothesis is denoted by $H_1$. When sample statistics do not support the null hypothesis, we can say that the alternative hypothesis is true.

### 8.4.3   *Type I and Type II Errors*

According to Akobeng (2016), there are two types of errors that are found in case of hypothesis testing. The first error occurs if the null hypothesis gets rejected, when it is true. It is called a Type I error that is denoted by

*Table 8.1* Type I and Type II errors

|  | *Accept $H_0$* | *Reject $H_0$* |
| --- | --- | --- |
| **$H_0$ (True)** | Correct | Type I error ($\alpha$ error) |
| **$H_0$ (False)** | Type II error ($\beta$ error) | Correct |

$\alpha$ (alpha). The second error occurs when the null hypothesis is accepted, when it is false. It is called as a Type II error which is denoted by $\beta$ (beta).

## 8.5 Descriptive Statistics

Descriptive statistics refers to numbers that produce a concise summary of the data. Summarised data may be in numerical or graphical form. Descriptive statistics helps to describe and analyse the data in a meaningful way for a research study. It is very useful to represent the raw data for explaining the research objectives. Fisher and Marshall (2009) opined descriptive analyses to be the simplest when it comes to both application as well as interpretation. We have discussed some of the popular techniques used in descriptive statistics here.

### 8.5.1 Measures of Central Tendency

Measurement of central tendency indicates the central value of a frequency distribution in a research data. It evaluates the average value of the sample. According to Manikandan (2011a, 2011b), the objective of measures of central tendency is to present an accurate description of the entire data. The commonly used measures of central tendency are mentioned below:

- **Mathematical average**
  - *Arithmetic mean* is obtained by adding all the observations and then dividing it by the number of observations.
  - *Geometric mean* is calculated as the $n$th root of the multiplication of all the n values of the research variable. It is relevant for the large items in a data series.
  - *Harmonic mean* is obtained by dividing the number of observations by the reciprocal of each value in the data series. It is used for evaluating the averages that include price, ratio, speed, and time.
- **Positional average**
  - *Median* is the middle point of the series in which half the values are less than and half the values are greater than that point.
  - *Mode* indicates the highest frequency of the series.

### 8.5.2   *Measures of Spread*

Measures of spread describe the presence of homogeneity and heterogeneity in a set of data. Nick (2007) opined that a researcher is always interested in the amount of variability, or spread, present in the given set of observations. To determine this, following are used:

*   *Range* is computed by evaluating the difference between the highest and the lowest values in a data set.
*   *Interquartile range* is the difference between the upper and the lower quartiles in a data set.
*   *Standard deviation* which is the root mean square deviation measures the spread of a data set. The larger standard deviation indicates the more spread over the observations in the data set.

## 8.6   Correlation and Regression Analysis

Correlation and regression analysis describe the nature of relationships among the variables. Correlation analysis evaluates the relationship between a dependent and independent variable or among two independent variables. Whereas, regression analysis computes the relationship between a dependent and one or more independent variables. According to Shi and Conrad (2009), correlation analysis measures the strength of the linear relationship between two variables. In case of a positive correlation, one variable increases with the increase of another variable. However, in a negative correlation, one variable increases with the decrease of another variable. Regression analysis deals with the methods responsible for carrying out modelling of numerical data.

### 8.6.1   *Pearson's Product-Moment Correlation*

The Pearson product-moment correlation coefficient is denoted by 'r'. According to Mukaka (2012), it is used when both variables under the study are distributed normally. It evaluates the strength of a linear association among the two variables by drawing a line of best fit with the help of the data of two variables. In other words, Pearson correlation coefficient helps to locate the data points with reference to the line of best fit.

### *Karl Pearson's coefficient of correlation*

This quantitative measure indicates the degree of relationship between two variables. It is universally denoted by 'r'. If the variables are X and

Y, then Karl Pearson's Coefficient of correlation can be expressed as follows:

$$r = \frac{\sum \left( X - \bar{X} \right) \left( Y - \bar{Y} \right)}{\sqrt{\sum X - \bar{X})^2} \sqrt{(Y - \bar{Y})^2}}$$

where, $\bar{X}$ = mean of X variable and $\bar{Y}$ = mean of Y variable.

### 8.6.2   Characteristics of Correlation Coefficient

Giri and Biswas (2019) suggested the following characteristics of correlation coefficient:

- The correlation coefficient can only be evaluated for quantitative data.
- The correlation coefficient (r) must lie between −1 and +1.
- Positive value of 'r' indicates a positive relationship between the variables, that is, the variables shift in a similar direction, the negative value of 'r' indicates a negative relationship between the variables, that is, the variables shift in the opposite direction.
- It does not vary with the change of origin, scale, and units of measurement.
- Sometimes, it can mislead the research in the presence of more outliers or nonlinear relationships between variables. It cannot describe curved relationships because it is influenced by outliers. So, we need to check the scatter plot.

### 8.6.3   Linear Regression

Linear regression is the ensuing step after correlation. It is used to predict the influence of a variable (independent variable) on the other variable (dependent variable). In linear regression analysis, we deal with one dependent and one independent variable. According to Shi and Conrad (2009), linear regression includes either a single independent variable or multiple with two or more independent variables. If there are two or more independent variables, multiple regression is considered. A linear regression equation is expressed as follows:

$$Y = a + bx$$

where, Y = dependent variable; a = Y intercept, that is, intercept along y-axis; b = regression coefficient of Y on X; X = independent variable.

The intercept, or 'a', is equal to the value of y if the value of x is equal to zero.

### 8.6.4 Multiple Regression Analysis

Multiple regression analysis is executed by two or more independent variables and at least one dependent variable. It is used to test the impact of independent variables on dependent variables. Fisher (1980) considered multiple regression analysis to be extremely important for the accurate estimation of the effects of different factors on a specific variable. A multiple regression equation can be defined as follows:

$$Y = a + b_1 X_1 + b_2 X_2 + b_3 X_3 + \ldots + b_n X_n$$

Here, Y is the dependent variable and 'a' is the regression constant estimation. $b_1, b_2, b_3, \ldots b_n$ are the regression coefficient estimations of 'n' number of independent variables $X_1, X_2, X_3, \ldots X_n$.

## 8.7 Statistical Tests

There are different statistical tests on the basis of the study. These tests are particularly important in the testing of hypotheses that are made regarding the significance of a sample. We will discuss about some of these common tests here.

### 8.7.1 t-Tests

McLarty and Bahna (2009) found t-test to be the most popular statistical test. It investigates if there is a significant variance between the averages of two groups. These groups may share some similar characteristics. It is used when the researcher is not aware of the mean and standard deviation of the population. t-Tests can be classified into the following types:

- *One sample t-test* is used to determine if there is a difference in the averages of sample and population.
- *Independent sample t-test* compares the averages of two different groups.
- *Paired sample t-test* compares the average of the same group at different times.

### 8.7.2 Analysis of Variance

Analysis of variance (ANOVA) is used to test the equality of means of the samples drawn from more than two populations. It can inspect one or more variables that have an impact on the dependent variable. Also, it can test the differences in different groups under each variable. The dependent variable must be in interval or ratio scale and independent variables must be on nominal scale. The main assumption for ANOVA is that samples must be collected from the normal population with equal variance. Ståhle and Wold (1989) opined that only well-designed experiments hold the key for the successful implementation of ANOVA. It is generally applied in the following ways:

- *One-way ANOVA (completely randomised design)* is used in the case of one dependent variable (must be in interval or ratio scale) and one independent variable (must be in nominal scale) with various groups. It facilitates examining the equality of means of two or more groups under the independent variable.
- *Two-way ANOVA (randomised block design)* is used for one dependent variable (must be in interval or ratio scale) and two independent variables (must be in nominal scale) with various groups. The attribute of randomised block design is that each block is having an equal number of treatments.
- *Factorial design* is used for one dependent variable (must be in interval or ratio scale) and two or more independent variables (must be in nominal scale). Here, researchers can examine the associations between different variables. A number of associations can be evaluated by multiplying the number of groups of different independent variables.

### 8.7.3 Chi-Square Test

According to Tallarida and Murray (1987), chi-square test is applied to instances where experimental and theoretical frequencies are compared with each other on the basis of a hypothesis. The test is used for comparing the categorical variables as well as hypothesis testing of two categorical variables from a single population. It helps to determine if there is a significant relationship between the two categorical variables. Both Discrete and continuous data can be used in this case. Continuous data must be converted to definite categorical data prior to use in this test. Chi-square is denoted by $\chi^2$ which is always greater than ($>$) or equal to ($=$) zero. It can be mathematically expressed as follows:

$$\chi^2 = \sum \frac{(O-E)^2}{E}$$

where, O = observed score and E = expected score.

## 8.8 Factor Analysis

According to Giri and Biswas (2019), there may be a large number of variables in a research study to fulfil the research objectives. In data analysis, the presence of a large number of variables may create some inconvenience. Therefore, factor analysis which is a multivariate method is used to decrease a large number of variables to a few convenient ones. These extracted factors describe a major part of the variations of data. All interrelated variables are clubbed together to create independent factors. Factor analysis cannot identify whether the variable is dependent or independent. Generally, a 5- or 7-point Likert scale is used for collecting data through survey research. In some cases, it is difficult to understand the individual influence of the independent variable on the dependent variable if independent factors are correlated with each other. It is called a multi-collinearity problem. Factor analysis always uses interval or ratio scale data.

## References

Acharya, A. S., Prakash, A., Saxena, P., & Nigam, A. (2013). Sampling: Why and how of it. *Indian Journal of Medical Specialties, 4*(2), 330–333.

Akobeng, A. K. (2016). Understanding type I and type II errors, statistical power and sample size. *Acta Paediatrica, 105*(6), 605–609.

Anupama, K. (2018). Hypothesis types and research. *International Journal of Nursing Science Practice and Research, 4*(2), 78–80.

Fisher, F. M. (1980). Multiple regression in legal proceedings. *Columbia Law Review, 80*(4), 702–736.

Fisher, M. J., & Marshall, A. P. (2009). Understanding descriptive statistics. *Australian Critical Care, 22*(2), 93–97.

Giri, A., & Biswas, D. (2019). *Research methodology for social sciences*. New Delhi: SAGE Publications.

Hox, J. J., & Boeije, H. R. (2005). Data collection, primary versus secondary. In *Encyclopedia of social measurement* (Vol. 1, p. 593). Amsterdam: Elsevier.

Manikandan, S. (2011a). Measures of central tendency: Median and mode. *Journal of Pharmacology and Pharmacotherapeutics, 2*(3), 214.

Manikandan, S. (2011b). Measures of central tendency: The mean. *Journal of Pharmacology and Pharmacotherapeutics, 2*(2), 140.

McLarty, J. W., & Bahna, S. L. (2009). Statistical tests for 1 or 2 samples. *Annals of Allergy, Asthma & Immunology, 103*(4), S26–S30.

Mukaka, M. M. (2012). A guide to appropriate use of correlation coefficient in medical research. *Malawi Medical Journal, 24*(3), 69–71.

Nick, T. G. (2007). Descriptive statistics. In W. T. Ambrosius (Eds.), *Topics in biostatistics*. Methods in Molecular Biology™ (Vol. 404). New Jersey: Humana Press.

Pokhariyal, G. P. (2019). Importance of moderating and intervening variables on the relationship between independent and dependent variables. *International Journal of Statistics and Applied Mathematics, 4*(5), 1–4.

Sharma, G. (2017). Pros and cons of different sampling techniques. *International Journal of Applied Research, 3*(7), 749–752.

Shi, R., & Conrad, S. A. (2009). Correlation and regression analysis. *Ann Allergy Asthma Immunol, 103*(4), S34–S41.

Ståhle, L., & Wold, S. (1989). Analysis of variance (ANOVA). *Chemometrics and Intelligent Laboratory Systems, 6*(4), 259–272.

Tallarida, R. J., & Murray, R. B. (1987). Chi-square test. In *Manual of pharmacologic calculations* (pp. 140–142). New York: Springer.

# 9    Legal Issues and Legislation

The understanding of the legal aspects of business plays a major role in the overall management of the business. As all businesses are regulated by the legal framework, so a sound knowledge of basic laws is an asset for an entrepreneur. Thus, legal understanding is required for both aspiring as well as experienced entrepreneurs alike. It is noticed that entrepreneurs are proactive about handling the marketing and financial aspects of the business. However, due to multidimensional entrepreneurial activities, often the legal implications of business get overlooked. At times, it becomes essential to seek legal expertise in certain matters to ensure the smooth running of the business. We will discuss some of these aspects with reference to India, that an entrepreneur should be aware of in a business.

## 9.1    Types of Business

An entrepreneur should be aware of the nature and structure of the business he/she operates, that is, Sole Proprietorship, Private Limited, Limited Liability Limited, and so on. This is important as each type of business comes with its own legal obligations that affects the overall mission and vision of the business. Khanka (2006) suggested some of the common forms of business prevalent in India.

### 9.1.1    Sole Proprietorship

This is much sought after by entrepreneurs who have just started and are with limited capital. It is owned and controlled by a single person. Naidu (2010) described some important features of sole proprietorship:

- The Government registration should only be done which is pertinent to the particular business. There are no other separate registrations involved. Hence, the form of business can start within ten days in case the legal procedure is duly followed.

- The business holder has unlimited liability towards the payment of all the debts because there is no separate existence of a sole proprietorship.

### 9.1.2 Private Limited Company

This form of business is also in great demand for creation of new start-ups. Ghuman (2010) highlighted some of the following features of private limited companies:

- It allows raising of funds from outside sources easily by allowing the investors to become shareholders of the company as a board member of directors.
- There is a limited liability of the shareholders regarding the debt payment based on certain conditions.
- The credibility of this form of business is higher due greater legal compliances such as conduct of regular board meetings and filing annual returns to the Ministry of Corporate Affairs (MCA).

### 9.1.3 Limited Liability Partnership

According to Prasanna (2010), following characteristics of limited liability partnership (LLP) makes it popular among the entrepreneurs.

- It is less expensive to start a business under LLP, with far less compliances compared to a private limited company.
- There are limited liabilities of the partners that also offers a certain degree of protection with respect to the contributions made.
- A desired form for the start-ups which do not have the requirement of equity funding. There are also specific tax benefits provided.

In the table given below, we have presented a comparative analysis of some of the popular forms of business prevalent in India.

## 9.2 Intellectual Property Rights

IPR in the form of copyrights, patents, trademarks, and so on provides a means of legal protection and also enables the original creator to earn financial benefit, recognition, and rights over his/her creation or invention. Sharma (2014) opined that IPRs helps to create an environment that encourages creativity and innovation. A proper understanding of IPR helps an entrepreneur to protect his/her intellectual assets. The various forms of IPR are mentioned here.

*Table 9.1* Types of business

| Legal details | Proprietorship | Private limited company | LLP |
| --- | --- | --- | --- |
| **Legal status** | Not a separate legal entity. The promoter is accountable for all legal liabilities | A separate legal entity. Promoters aren't accountable for the liabilities | A separate legal entity. Promoters aren't accountable for the liabilities |
| **Registration** | Not needed | Required with the MCA under the Companies Act, 2013 | Required with MCA under the LLP Act, 2008 |
| **Required number of members** | Only one person (sole proprietor) | Minimum one person | Minimum two persons |
| **Member liability** | Unlimited | Limited, depending on the extent of the contribution | Limited, depending on the extent of the contribution |
| **Transferability** | Non-transferrable | Transferrable by means of share transfer | Transferrable |
| **Taxation applicable** | Individual taxation rules | Income Tax Act, 1961 guidelines alongside surcharge and cess | Income Tax Act, 1961 guidelines alongside surcharge and cess |
| **Annual filings** | Only income tax returns | Tax returns plus an annual statement of returns and solvency is to be filed with the registrar of the companies | Tax returns plus an annual statement of returns and solvency is to be filed with the registrar of the companies |
| **Annual statutory meetings** | Not mandatory | Periodic board and general meetings must be held | Not mandatory |
| **Foreign ownership** | Not allowed | Allowed with the prior permission of Reserve Bank of India and other applicable government permissions | Allowed with the prior permission of Reserve Bank of India and other applicable government permissions |

Source: Adapted from Startup India, Govt. of India

## *9.2.1   Copyright*

Under Indian laws, copyright is the protection that is granted to the original creators of a work. With the widespread internet accessibility these days, copyright has become increasingly important to download music, videos, literary work, and so forth. Entrepreneurs should have knowledge about this as any violation can lead to potential legal battles.

### 9.2.2   Patent

Patents are exclusive rights given to the original inventor over his/her invention which enables the exclusive commercial use of his/her invention for a limited period. It also helps in the prevention of any unauthorised use. An entrepreneur must be careful of not infringing on the patents of anyone else as it may result in potential legal complications. In India, the Indian Patent Act, 1970 governs the matters related to patents in the country.

### 9.2.3   Trademark

A trademark is an indicator that helps to identify distinct goods or services. It helps an entrepreneur to differentiate his/her offerings from those of other entities. It can be of any form, for example, sign, logo, and so on, which gives the offerings a unique identity.

### 9.2.4   Trade Secret

According to Khanka (2006), a trade secret refers to classified details, production methods, design, and so on which is not revealed and helps the business to attain a competitive advantage in the market. It can last as long as it remains a secret. The entrepreneur has the choice of either maintaining secrecy of his/her idea or monetises it as a trade secret.

Moreover, an entrepreneur should also be aware about the following matters which are essential for the sustainability of the venture and will also ensure peace of mind.

* *Licensing* refers to the mutual agreement where a company issues license to another company to the temporal access of IPRs, manufacturing process, branding, trade secret, and so on of the former under specified conditions. Licensing is a marketing strategy often employed by companies to venture into markets where they lack reach, resources, and experience.
* *Insurance* acts as an envelope or cover in the event of future risks. It provides a means to mitigate the chances of mishaps associated with a venture. There are various types of insurances depending on the requirements of the entrepreneur. Hence, there should be careful consideration before choosing an insurance plan. Insurance features prominently in the overall financial planning of an enterprise as it helps to determine the cost projections.

- *Product safety and liability* mandates the manufacturing of a product should be in compliance with the Government laws related to safety and standardisation because of the concern for the safety and well-being of the end user. Entrepreneurs should ensure there is no violation especially those involved with hazardous or inflammable substances.

## 9.3    Legal Provisions and Legislation

In recent times, there has been a growing surge in the start-up space in the country. There is a strong inclination of the younger generation towards entrepreneurship. At the same time, entrepreneurs should also be aware of a wide gamut of legal provisions relating to working conditions, employee remuneration, medical benefits, and so forth. According to Parker (2007), there are two ways through which law and entrepreneurship comes in contact with each other. Legal mechanisms are responsible for determining the form of entrepreneurship in an organisation. It also plays a major role in the regulation, bankruptcy legislation, property rights, and so on in entrepreneurship. Some of the general provisions that an entrepreneur must keep in mind are discussed as follows:

- **Prevention of discriminatory practices**

  There should be no discrimination on the basis of gender, race, religion, caste, and place of birth when it comes to recruitment, selection, promotion, remuneration, and so on. The Government has strict laws to deal with any such violation at workplaces. Hence, the entrepreneurs should be aware and careful that no such issues arise at the workplace.

- **Overtime**

  An employee who works for more than the stipulated working hours in the specified industries is titled to receive overtime wages. However, it should be within the permissible guidelines such that employee's health is not affected. The overtime rate is two times the usual hourly rate of the worker.

- **Rest**

  In order to get the best output from the employees, the entrepreneur should ensure that the employees should be given adequate rest. As per the law, every employee who has worked for at least 240 days per year must be given 12 paid days of leave. Moreover, the employees are also titled to paid leaves on national holidays, that is, Republic Day, Independence Day, and Mahatma Gandhi's birthday.

- **Privacy**

  Employers have the right to make background checks on prospective employees. The information about the employees must be kept confidential. They can monitor the official communication and other matters related to the workplace. However, there should not be any kind of intrusion to the employee's personal communication and there are strict privacy laws in at place. All the company guidelines are to be mentioned in the appointment letter, employment agreements, and so forth, and the employees are also to be apprised about the same.

- **Termination notice**

  An employee must be given prior notification in case of termination or dismissal. The employee should be given a fair chance of defending his/her position if there is a disciplinary action.

Moreover, the bonus, gratuity, and other dues applicable are to be paid accordingly to that employee. An entrepreneur must build awareness about these to ensure the smooth running of the business.

Now, we will discuss in brief the certain provisions of the prominent labour laws applicable in India which an entrepreneur must be familiar with. **However, one should always refer to the authorised government sources for the comprehensive and latest because these are often subjected to amendments and updates**.

### 9.3.1   The Payment of Wages Act, 1936

This Act regulates the wage payment of specific classes of employees working in industry. It prescribes the wage payment to be made in certain form at regular intervals without any unwarranted deductions. The act envisages the following guidelines:

- The maximum wage period may not exceed one month.
- Within ten days of the month end, wages should be paid. However, the wages are to be paid within 7 days of month end in case of industrial establishments with less than 1000 employees working.
- Every employer is supposed to maintain records/registers which should record the information regarding the work performed, wages paid, deductions made, receipts, and so on about each of its employees. Moreover, these records are to be preserved for at least three years from the date of last entry.

### 9.3.2 The Industrial Employment (Standing Orders) Act, 1946

The Act aims to preserve the industrial harmony through the regulation of employment terms and conditions such as recruitment, leaves, discharge of duties, and so forth for the employees working in specified industrial establishments. Some of the important features of the Act are mentioned below:

- The Act mandates the industrial establishments to define the employment conditions and make their employees aware of the same.
- The Act applies to industrial establishments where no less than 100 workmen are employed or were employed on any day in the previous 12 months.
- Earlier Software & IT industry in India was given exemption from complying with this act for 11 years. However, after 2012, all the Software & IT companies which employ more than 100 employees also fall under the ambit of this act.
- The Act has laid down guidelines regarding the classification of workmen (permanent, temporary, apprentices, etc.), hours of work, holidays, pay-days, and wage rates.
- The Act also envisages the guidelines about the matters related to the termination of employment, notice period, suspension, or dismissal for misconduct and means of redressal for workmen grievances.

### 9.3.3 The Minimum Wages Act, 1948

This Act is based on the principle of social justice which aims to protect the vulnerable workmen against forms of exploitation. It statutorily provides minimum wage rates for workers engaged in specified schedule employments. Some important features of the Act are as given below:

- Minimum wage threshold can be set up by both the Centre as well as States.
- This is a statutory act which is not legally binding. However, any form of employment wherein employee is paid below minimum wages will be treated as forced labour. It will also be considered a statutory non-compliance.
- Minimum wage rates vary across the country and the entrepreneur must be careful about the applicable local minimum wage rates.

### 9.3.4 *The Employees' State Insurance Act, 1948*

This Act is in place to provide financial benefits regarding sickness, work-place injuries, and other medical exigencies to the employees under the following conditions.

- The Act applies to establishments that employ no less than ten employees and the monthly wages of the beneficiaries do not exceed ₹21,000/-.
- The Employees' State Insurance (ESI) fund is made up of the contributions made by both employer and employee. The contribution of employers and employees is 4.75 percent and 1.75 percent of the total wages, respectively. Employee contribution is exempted in case the employee wages are less than ₹100/- per day.

### 9.3.5 *The Factories Act, 1948*

The main objective of the Act is to limit the extension of undirected factories and securing requisite protection measures for the wellbeing of the factory workers. The Act covers aspects such as working hours, breaks, employing young adults, and provisions related to hazardous processes. The Act applies to factories,

- Where manufacturing process (refers to making and repairing of products, power generation, printing activities, ship-building, or cold storage) is carried out with the aid of power and no less than ten employees are working or were working on any day in the previous 12 months, or
- Where manufacturing process is carried out without the aid of power and no less than 20 employees are working or were working on any day in the previous 12 months.

### 9.3.6 *The Employees' Provident Fund and Miscellaneous Provisions Act, 1952*

The Act gives a form of social security to the employees. It imparts retirement benefits in the form of provident fund, insurance linked to deposits, pension, and so on. Some of the key features of the Act are as follows:

- The Act mandates organisations with 20 or more employees to register for the EPF scheme.
- Both the employer and employee contribute 12 percent of the basic plus dearness allowance towards the EPF account which acts as the retirement fund of an employee.

- EPF contributions are mandatory for employees who earn basic wages up to ₹15,000 per month.

### 9.3.7    *The Maternity Benefit Act, 1961*

The Act regulates the employment of women regarding childbirth. It mandates the employer to impart prescribed maternity benefits in the form of maternity leave, wages, and so forth.

- The Act applies to female employees employed in establishments not covered under ESI Act, 1948 and also to those who are not eligible to be covered under it.
- The Act authorises every female employee a leave of not exceeding 12 weeks alongside the payment of maternity benefit at the rate of her daily average wages.
- In order to be eligible for this benefit, a female employee must have worked for a minimum period of 80 days in the previous 12 months.

### 9.3.8    *The Payment of Bonus Act, 1965*

The Act prescribes paying of bonus to the employees employed in specified establishments based on its profits and productivity. The Act applies to establishments that employ no less than 20 people.

The payment of a bonus is subjected to the following conditions:

- During the accounting year, the employee must have worked for no less than 30 days.
- The salary of the employee should not exceed ₹21,000.
- The minimum bonus payable must be 8.33 percent of annual wages.
- The bonus is to be calculated at a monthly wage of ₹7,000 or the minimum wages applicable, whichever is higher.
- The payment of bonus should be made within a period not exceeding eight months from the completion of an accounting year.

### 9.3.9    *The Contract Labour (Regulation & Abolition) Act, 1970*

The Act aims to obstruct ill treatment of contract labour through introduction of healthy working conditions. The Act is applicable to:

- Every establishment in which 20 or more workmen are employed or were employed as contract labour on any day in the previous 12 months.
- Every contractor who employs or employed 20 or more workmen on any day in the previous 12 months.

Under this Act, the principal employer is responsible for providing rest-rooms, washing facilities, first aid, timely payment of wages, and so on, to the contract labour.

### 9.3.10 The Payment of Gratuity Act, 1972

The Act is intended to provide monetary benefits after retirement and is applicable to employees working in railways, ports, factories, mines, oil-fields, and plantations wherein no less than ten persons are employed or were employed in the previous 12 months.

- Gratuity is a mandatory payment to be made to an employee upon the termination of service, provided the employee has had a continuous service of not less than five years.
- The payment of gratuity is calculated at the rate of 15 days per year of service for every completed year of service based on the last drawn salary. Gratuity must be paid within 30 days of the last working day of the employee.

### 9.3.11 The Sexual Harassment of Women at Workplace (Prevention, Prohibition, and Redressal) Act, 2013

The Act aims to safeguard women against sexual harassment at the work-place. The workplace also includes the external facilities provided to perform the work such as transportation, cafeteria, and so on. Some of the important features under the Act are follows:

- The Act is applicable to both organised as well as unorganised sectors including public and private organisations. It covers regular, temporary, and contractual employees.
- As per the Act, any interference or creating a hostile work environment that can affect the safety, morale or health of a female employee may be treated as sexual harassment.
- The Act mandates an employer to set up an 'Internal Complaints Committee (ICC)' in establishments with no less than ten employees. It is authorised to make suggestions to the employer, at the behest of the aggrieved employee also in the form of ad hoc measures like transfer or leave of the aggrieved woman.
- The Act prescribes complaint redressal to be completed in a time-bound manner. A penalty of up to ₹50,000 can be levied if the employer fails to form ICC or fails to comply with any of the provisions under the Act.

*Table 9.2* MSME definitions

|  | Micro enterprise | Small enterprise | Medium enterprise |
| --- | --- | --- | --- |
| **Manufacturing** (investment in plant and machinery) | Investment up to ₹25 lakhs | Investment over ₹25 lakhs to ₹5 crores | Investment over ₹5 crores to ₹10 crores |
| **Services** (investment in equipment) | Investment up to ₹10 lakhs | Investment over ₹10 lakhs to ₹2 crores | Investment over ₹2 crores to ₹5 crores |

### 9.3.12    *The MSMEs Development Act, 2006*

The Act aims to foster and intensify the growth of MSMEs. It is considered to be a graded step regarding formally defining MSMEs. Some of the key provisions under the Act are as follows:

* The legal framework towards recognition of 'enterprise' comprising both manufacturing and service establishments is provided by the Act.
* The Act also specifically described the medium enterprises as MSMEs with clearly defined parameters.
* The Central Government is empowered to take up relevant programmes aimed to enhance and develop the MSMEs.

The MSMEs (Amendment) Bill, 2015 has proposed certain changes in the MSMEs Development Act, 2006. The Bill calls for extending the investment limits regarding setting up of plant and machinery in micro, small and medium enterprises.

In this chapter, we have discussed legal issues and some of the labour laws applicable in India. The aim was to give the learners a basic idea about the same. However, the authors strongly advise the readers to go through the authorised government sources for legislation as these are subjected to revisions, amendments and updates.

### References

The Contract Labour (Regulation and Abolition) Act, 1970.
The Employees' Provident Fund and Miscellaneous Provisions Act, 1952.
The Employees' State Insurance Act, 1948.
The Factories Act, 1948.
Ghuman, K. (2010). *Management: Concepts, practice & cases.* New Delhi: Tata McGraw Hill Education.

The Indian Patent Act, 1970.

The Industrial Employment (Standing Orders) Act, 1946.

Khanka, S. S. (2006). *Entrepreneurial development*. New Delhi: S. Chand Publishing.

The Maternity Benefit Act, 1961.

The Micro, Small and Medium Enterprises Development Act, 2006.

The Minimum Wages Act, 1948.

Naidu, N. V. R. (2010). *Management and entrepreneurship*. New Delhi: IK International Pvt Ltd.

Parker, S. C. (2007). Law and the economics of entrepreneurship. *Comparative Labor Law and Policy Journal, 28*(4), 695–716.

The Payment of Bonus Act, 1965.

The Payment of Gratuity Act, 1972.

The Payment of Wages Act, 1936.

Prasanna, C. (2010). *Fundamentals of financial management*. New Delhi: Tata McGraw Hill Education.

The Sexual Harassment of Women at Workplace Act, 2013.

Sharma, D. K. (2014). Intellectual property and the need to protect it. *Indian Journal of Scientific Research, 9*(1), 84–87.

Types of Businesses. Retrieved August 19, 2020, from www.startupindia.gov.in/content/sih/en/international/go-to-market-guide/types-of-businesses.html

# 10  Cases on Entrepreneurship

Entrepreneurship development has tremendous scope for growth and development. In the last decade, India has emerged to be the hotspot of successful entrepreneurial ventures. The vast majority of these entrepreneurs are from families with no background in business. Case studies present an overview of the enterprise and help to analyse the reasons in making the success or failure of a business. We have presented some cases of entrepreneurship in India based on innovation, grit, and determination.

## Case 1: The Success Story of Project Sukanya

Aparna Banerjee, a Kolkata-based social entrepreneur founded a retail chain called 'Project Sukanya' in the year 2005. She is an alumnus of XLRI, a prestigious business school in India. The business model is based on the systematic integration of rural vendors and urban end users. The retail chain under the project is constituted by mobile kiosks. The unique project aims to meet the social responsibility obligations alongside attaining the core business interests. Under the project, skilled women mostly from weaker sections of the society are provided a platform to sell homemade items and handicrafts through efficient training and management. Aparna started working on the concept from 1996, when she envisaged to impart required marketing and entrepreneurial support to women and rural entrepreneurs under a sole banner. Her management degree helped her to understand that inferior marketing strategies act as key barriers to the growth and success of women and rural entrepreneurs. There is limited awareness about the importance of brand visibility among these entrepreneurs. This is the reason that the 'Project Sukanya' has given special emphasis to this aspect. The kiosks are designed to catch the attention that are strategically located across the city. These kiosks are branded as 'Bou' (means women in Bengali language) are serviced by apron-clad women. These kiosks are recognised for their committed service and professionalism. The project aims to build a brand image for the products of cottage industries. It markets gift items, spices, potato chips, sarees, fruits, and so on under the brand name 'Sukanya'. Moreover, the edible products are tested and authenticated by National Test House, a Government of India body. The products as well as the packaging are ensured to maintain the highest quality standards. The women who are associated with the project strive to build a long-term relationship with the customers by offering coherent services. The project has registered healthy growth and is becoming popular in other parts of India as well.

The case is adapted from the following sources:

Banerjee, S., & Dasgupta, P. (2009). Branding in small and medium enterprises: A conceptual model to manage branding initiatives. In 1st International Conference of the Society for Global Business & Economic Development, at Bratislava, Slovak Republic.

Mitra, R. (2020, April 23). Helping women turn entrepreneurs. Retrieved August 09, 2020, from www.femina.in/women/women-like-you/helping-women-turn-entrepreneurs-224 6.html

The Hindu BusinessLine. (2011, January 22). Manned by women. Retrieved August 09, 2020, from www.thehindubusinessline.com/todays-paper/tp-life/Manned-by-women/article 20015405.ece

## Case 2: SuperProcure: A Disruptor in Logistics

India ranks 35th in the World Bank's Logistics Performance Index. It highlights the low efficiency of logistics in India. In spite of the presence of several players, there is an ample scope of improvement in the domain. With the aim of bringing innovation and disruption in the logistics market in the country, Anup Agarwal, Varun Biyani and Manisha Saraf joined hands to found a SaaS-based start-up named SuperProcure in the year 2017 in Kolkata. It works to bring down the logistics expenses through optimisation and digitisation of logistics as well as supply chain management. The software is tailor-made to automate the important business operations that include floating of requirements and taking quotes from the transporters which helps to take the final call regarding the daily dispatch allocation. Moreover, the product offered also has a built-in reverse auction engine to enable the freight negotiation to be fully computerised. SuperProcure is focused towards bringing transparency and reliability in the logistics workflow with real-time communication and coordination. The platform offers a 100 percent audit-compliant process by maintaining data about each action executed on the platform during freight negotiation. The automation of workflow has resulted in the improvement of productivity for each of the stakeholders— owner, transporter, and end user. This has also helped them to raise profit margins and revenue. Initially, SuperProcure had started its operations with only five customers. Today, it boasts of diversified clients dealing in manufacturing, fast-moving consumer goods, infrastructure development that include the likes of LNTECC, Tata Global Beverage, Godrej Agrovet, Borosil, PepsiCo, Jain Irrigation, Shyam Steel, Dukes India, and so forth. From the beginning itself, founders were convinced about the presence of huge potential in the logistics space. A revamp in logistics is required in the similar lines of accounting and marketing when SAP, Tally, Salesforce, and so on were first introduced 30 years ago. SuperProcure has received seed investment support from Indian Institute of Management Calcutta Innovation Park. The revenue is generated through charging one-time licensing, customisation, and implementation fees alongside charging subscription fees for recurring transactions. It has witnessed considerable growth. The revenue has doubled in the last 12 months, and it aspires to expand into global markets. SuperProcure has been recognised for bringing the much-required innovation and disruption in the logistics space. It has bagged several awards from CII, NASSCOM, and many more.

The case is adapted from the following sources:

About Us: SuperProcure: Logistics Management System. (2020, June 09). Retrieved September 10, 2020, from www.superprocure.com/about-us/
Kashyaap, S. (2019, December 13). This Kolkata-based logistics startup helps with seamless daily freight, reduced spends. Retrieved September 10, 2020, from https://yourstory.com/ 2019/12/kolkata-based-logistics-startup-superprocure

## Case 3: Lijjat Papad: A Unique Case of Women Entrepreneurship

'Papad' is a crunchy bread widely consumed in Indian households as a snack. There are several companies who are involved in the manufacturing, selling, and distribution of papads in India. However, during the early years of independence, there was a dearth of quality papads. To address this, a group of seven women Jaswantiben Jamnadas Popat, Parvatiben Ramdas Thodani, Ujamben Narandas Kundalia, Banuben. N. Tanna, Laguben Amritlar Gokani, and Jayaben V. Vithalani came together to start Shri Mahila Griha Udyog Lijjat Papad (SMGULP) as a micro enterprise in the year 1959 in Bombay (now Mumbai) with the combined investment of ₹80. Since its inception, SMGULP emphasised on women empowerment, building mutual trust, and creating quality products. In the initial years, it was mentored by Chaganlal Karamsi Parkeh who stressed on the importance of maintaining a coherent distribution and supply chain. The group had a unique concept of working on the basis of membership instead of ownership where the profits are distributed equitably. Today, there are 21 core members managing the operations of SMGULP with its widespread presence across India. Each branch is administered by a team of 11 members, known as '*Sanchaliks*'. The brand name '*Lijjat*' means tasty in Gujarati language. Positive word of mouth, television commercials, and coverage in local newspapers had brought immense popularity to the brand. To give a unique identity to the brand Lijjat Bunny, a mascot was introduced. The company also tried to expand the business by offering detergent powders, soaps, and so on by creating a separate brand '*Sasa*'. Although it had started as a micro enterprise with seven members but today, the annual turnover exceeds ₹300 crores alongside a significant export revenue. There are more than 40,000 employees working in the company. SMGULP, with its humble beginnings has become a classic example of success stories of SMEs in India with the core objective of women empowerment.

The case is adapted from the following sources:

Banerjee, S., & Dasgupta, P. (2009). Branding in small and medium enterprises: A conceptual model to manage branding initiatives. In 1st International Conference of the Society for Global Business & Economic Development, at Bratislava, Slovak Republic.
Lijjat Homepage. Retrieved August 11, 2020, from www.lijjat.com/

## Case 4: iKure: Transforming the Rural Healthcare

There is a serious dearth of quality health care in the rural and far-flung areas of India with immense scope of application of technology in the sector. iKure, founded by Sujay Santra in 2010, a social venture aims to provide tech-based affordable primary health care which can be easily accessed by people alongside providing a platform in which the doctor-patient communication continues past the four walls of the clinic. iKure aspire to offer a community driven comprehensive healthcare through innovation, technology, and community health workers (CHWs). With an extensive network of health workers and hubs, it delivers health care to the last mile. iKure conducts regular healthcare camps regarding, eye screening, diabetes, maternal and child health, and so forth. It has also established a chain of health clinics with doctors and medical staff in remote areas without access to PHCs within the vicinity of 20 km. iKure is also engaged in the training of CHWs through its in-house patent pending software Wireless Health Incident Monitoring System (WHIMS) to collect, monitor, and analyse the patient data. The data are used for studying numerous endemic diseases prevalent in communities to develop comprehensive healthcare solutions for disease prevention through partnerships with NGOs, healthcare providers, and so on. The CHWs are also trained to deliver tailor-made quality healthcare services to the doorstep of patients. At present, WHIMS is operated in eight countries across the globe. It has been recognised as one of the Top 60 Innovations in the world by MIT Solve Judges. It has entered into several notable partnerships with University of Michigan, Deshpande Foundation, TATA Trust, and so forth. iKure is regarded as one of the pioneers in the development of the sustainable primary healthcare model in the world.

The case is adapted from the following sources:

Chaudhuri, A., Saddikutti, V., &Prætorius, T. (2018). iKureTechsoft: Providing Technology Enabled Affordable Health Care in Rural India. Asian Case Research Journal, 22(02), 385–411.
Touching Millions of Lives. Retrieved August 11, 2020, from www.ikure techsoft.com/

## Case 5: Chefrome: A Distinctive Food Tech Start-Up

Chefrome is an online food-tech company based in Kolkata. It delivers authentic home-cooked food to corporations and individuals. It was founded by Rizwan Zaman in 2018 with the aim of promoting micro-entrepreneurship among women who are passionate about cooking ('mom chefs') and aspire for financial independence. It was difficult for Rizwan to quit a well-paid job to invest in a start-up with limited resources. In his ten years of corporate experience, Rizwan always craved homemade food at work as he didn't like carrying tiffin to the workplace. The company began its operations with the intention of empowering women alongside encouraging healthy lifestyle amongst the working populace. It organises regular cooking workshops, contests, and so on for budding chefs. Chefrome functions as an aggregator of the home-cooked food and earns commission per order. It has a rigorous Chef on-boarding process to ensure continuous supply of food and optimum utilisation of the available resources. It employs both in-house delivery agents as well as third party delivery services. Initially, Chefrome started with one chef that has grown to 130 chefs. The team consists of five full-time members. Majority of the team members are young with degrees in engineering and management. At present, it provides services to more than 1000 customers spread around 30 corporate offices in Kolkata. It also offers home-cooked food to the parties, events, and festivals. Some of the key challenges faced by Rizwan were regarding customer acquisition, employee recruitment, uniformity of taste, and so forth. Chefrome applies a selective approach in customer acquisition which has helped to maintain positive net margin. Within such a short span of operations, the company has become profitable. The company believes in maintaining utmost transparency with all the stakeholders. In the near future, the company looks to expand its operations to other Indian metro cities. Chefrome has received a lot of accolades for its unique concept. It was amongst the Top 6 start-ups in Converge 2.0 at 13th International E-Summit which was organised by IIMC.

The case is adapted from the following source:

Vivek. (2020, July 03). Rizwan's Chefrome—Authentic Home-Cooked food for all. Retrieved August 11, 2020, from www.hrdots.com/chefrome-authentic-home-cooked-food/

# Glossary

**Agricultural Entrepreneur**  An agricultural entrepreneur engages in activities related to agriculture.

**Agricultural Entrepreneurship**  Agricultural entrepreneurship is concerned with the marketing and production of products based on agriculture.

**Appendix**  An appendix is the hindmost part of the document which contains additional information that is not included earlier.

**Business Entrepreneur**  A business entrepreneur comes up with an idea of a novel product or service and makes efforts to transform it into reality.

**Business Model**  A business model elucidates the key strategies an organisation undertakes to make profits.

**Business Plan**  A business plan is an active or ongoing document that outlines various sides of a particular business in the short- and long term to achieve business goals.

**Classical Entrepreneur**  A classical entrepreneur aims for profit maximisation through traditional means with or without the presence of any growth element.

**Corporate Entrepreneur**  A corporate entrepreneur applies innovative skills to manage a corporate undertaking.

**Digital Entrepreneurship**  Digital entrepreneurship describes the influence of digital technology on entrepreneurship.

**Direct Cost**  Cost that directly takes part in production or involved in the core business activities, e.g., labour, material.

**Drone Entrepreneur**  A drone entrepreneur is identified as rigid and conventional who discard new techniques in spite of lesser profits.

**Entrepreneur**  A person who is engaged in a business and also undertakes the risks associated with it.

**Entrepreneurship**  The competence of an entrepreneur who applies innovative techniques in the way a business is conducted.

**Entrepreneurial Culture** The cultural attributes which encourage an individual to take up entrepreneurship and make a living out of it.

**Entrepreneurial Potential** The perceived desirability and propensity of an individual to create a business.

**Entrepreneurial Society** The society which fosters the practice of entre-preneurship and gives recognition to the innovations introduced by entrepreneurs.

**Executive Summary** The component which summarises the business plan.

**Fabian Entrepreneur** A fabian entrepreneur is somewhat reluctant to experiment with new ways in their business.

**Finance** It is defined as the position of money at the time it is wanted.

**Financial Statement** It is a document that contains all the financial activities and helps us understand business financial performance.

**First Generation Entrepreneur** A first generation entrepreneur does not have any entrepreneurial background.

**Fixed Cost** The cost that will be used in the business irrespective of the sales volume or activity will be your fixed cost. This cost is fixed no matter what the business does.

**Fixed Capital** Capital invested in fixed assets.

**Funding** Funding is the process in which money is supplied by an institute or government, for a specific purpose.

**Growth Entrepreneur** A growth entrepreneur undertakes the necessary risk in a high growth industry.

**Health Entrepreneurship** Health entrepreneurship aims to build utility based digital healthcare products or services through implementation of innovative techniques.

**Imitative Entrepreneur** An imitative entrepreneur is always ready to embrace innovations in his/her business.

**Indirect Cost** Cost that is required to support the business-like rent, electricity, service charges, etc.

**Induced Entrepreneur** An induced entrepreneur takes up entrepreneurship because of the incentives and subsidies given by the Government.

**Industrial Entrepreneur** An industrial entrepreneur is focused on activities related to manufacturing and production.

**Inherited Entrepreneur** An entrepreneur who has inherited a family business or has gained experience from it.

**Innovative Entrepreneur** An innovative entrepreneur is mostly aggressive with a knack of transforming the possibilities into reality.

**Intrapreneur** An employee of the organisation who is paid according to the performance of the business under his/her responsibility.

**Manager** is the person who manages the operations and functions of the organisation.

**Marketing**   The action which involves the promotion of the business.

**Motivated Entrepreneur**   A motivated entrepreneur works towards reaching self-actualisation.

**Non-technical Entrepreneur**   A non-technical entrepreneur is focused on the activities related to marketing and distribution.

**Professional Entrepreneur**   A professional entrepreneur uses innovative ideas to set up a business but is not interested in its management or operations.

**Pure Entrepreneur**   A pure entrepreneur is driven by the financial rewards associated with a business.

**Retail Entrepreneurs**   A retail entrepreneur generally undertakes trading related activities.

**Rural Entrepreneurship**   The entrepreneurial activities which are carried out in rural areas with the aim of value creation to rural resources and involving largely the rural folk.

**Social Entrepreneurship**   The entrepreneurial activities which involves creation and implementation of unique solutions to the social and environmental concerns.

**Second Generation Entrepreneurs**   A second-generation entrepreneur inherits family business.

**Service Entrepreneur**   A service entrepreneur is one who provides services to customers.

**Social Entrepreneur**   A social entrepreneur is one who provides importance to the society by serving them.

**Spontaneous Entrepreneur**   A person turns out to be an entrepreneur, because of the natural talent vested in him.

**Start-ups**   A young business venture established to create a unique product or service with the help of a scalable business model.

**Super-growth Entrepreneur**   A super-growth entrepreneur shows high performance in their venture measured by high profits.

**SWOT Analysis**   S—Strength, W—Weakness, O—Opportunity, and T—Threat. This analysis helps to analyse the Internal and external factors that will address the business strategy.

**Technical Entrepreneur**   A technical entrepreneur is focused on activities related to technology and innovation.

**Trading Entrepreneur**   A trading entrepreneur undertakes activities related to trading and sales.

**Variable Cost**   The cost that will be incurred by the business due to its day-to-day activity is known as the variable cost. This cost depends on the day-to-day activity.

**Women Entrepreneur**   When women take initiative towards setting and managing a business.

**Women Entrepreneurship**   An enterprise that is owned and controlled by women where the majority of the financial interest are with women and also majority of employees are women.

**Working Capital**   The capital required to run daily business activities.

# Index

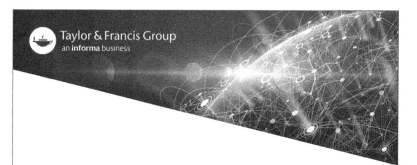